NORTHAMPTON'S TRAMS AND BUSES

A JOURNEY THROUGH TIME

DAVID BEDDALL

AN IMPRINT OF PEN & SWORD BOOKS LTD.
YORKSHIRE – PHILADELPHIA

First published in Great Britain in 2023 by
Pen and Sword Transport
An imprint of
Pen & Sword Books Ltd.
Yorkshire - Philadelphia

Copyright © David Beddall, 2023

ISBN 978 1 52678 096 6

The right of David Beddall to be identified as author of this work has been asserted by him in accordance with the Copyright, Designs and Patents Act 1988.

A CIP catalogue record for this book is available from the British Library.

All rights reserved. No part of this book may be reproduced or transmitted in any form or by any means, electronic or mechanical including photocopying, recording or by any information storage and retrieval system, without permission from the Publisher in writing.

Typeset by SJmagic DESIGN SERVICES, India.

Printed and bound in India by Replika Press Pvt. Ltd.

Pen & Sword Books Ltd incorporates the imprints of Pen & Sword Books Archaeology, Atlas, Aviation, Battleground, Discovery, Family History, History, Maritime, Military, Naval, Politics, Railways, Select, Transport, True Crime, Fiction, Frontline Books, Leo Cooper, Praetorian Press, Seaforth Publishing, Wharncliffe and White Owl.

For a complete list of Pen & Sword titles please contact

PEN & SWORD BOOKS LIMITED
47 Church Street, Barnsley, South Yorkshire, S70 2AS, England
E-mail: enquiries@pen-and-sword.co.uk
Website: www.pen-and-sword.co.uk

or

PEN AND SWORD BOOKS
1950 Lawrence Rd, Havertown, PA 19083, USA
E-mail: Uspen-and-sword@casematepublishers.com
Website: www.penandswordbooks.com

NORTHAMPTON'S TRAMS AND BUSES

A JOURNEY THROUGH TIME

I would like to dedicate this book to my son, Morris.

CONTENTS

Acknowledgements *6*

Introduction *7*

1880–1909 .... *10*

1910–1919 .... *12*

1920–1929 .... *18*

1930–1939 .... *32*

1940–1949 .... *45*

1950–1959 .... *49*

1960–1969 .... *80*

1970–1979 .... *85*

1980–1989 .... *91*

1990–1999 .... *102*

2000–2009 ....*113*

2010–2019 .... *121*

2020–2021 .... *128*

Sources *200*

ACKNOWLEDGEMENTS

My first thank you goes to my wife Helen and my son for their patience during the preparation of this book. A big thank you goes to Liam Farrer-Beddall, Gary Seamarks, David Hancock, Laurence Knight, Ben Everitt, David Moth, David Shadbolt, Matt Cooper, Simon Butler, Roger Warwick and Steve Loveridge and the 794 Preservation Group for allowing me to use images from their archives. Thank you also goes to Peter Waller of the Online Transport Archive for allowing me to use a number of images of Northampton Trams; as well as Kezlan Images and Michael Eyres for allowing me use of images from the J.S. Cockshott archive. Another thank you goes to the staff at The Bus Archive's Walsall library for their assistance during research of sections of this book.

INTRODUCTION

Northampton, the county town of Northamptonshire, lies on the river Nene. The market town can trace its history back to the Bronze Age, with Northampton being granted a town charter by Richard I in 1189. Today the town is located close to the M1 motorway, with the A45 trunk road passing through connecting to the A14 near Kettering. Northampton, along with Northamptonshire as a whole, is perhaps most famous for its shoe industry, with many shoe factories being located in the town. An industry dating back over 500 years, it went into rapid decline during the 1960s, with the British Shoe Corporation being partly responsible for this. The Corporation imported cheap shoes to the United Kingdom.

Northampton was similar to many towns and cities in the United Kingdom, expanding after the end of the First World War. Northampton expanded far beyond the termini of the tram network that had been introduced in the Victorian era. This led to the need for bus services in the Northampton area to pick up the shortfall. By the 1930s, Northampton's borough boundaries had expanded to incorporate Weston Favell, Duston, Dallington, Hardingstone, Boughton and Moulton Park. The post-war years saw further expansion of Northampton. In 1968 it was announced that Northampton would be included as a London overspill area, with an estimated 80,000 additional people living in the town by the mid-1980s. This led to the development of new housing estates in the east of the town, known as the Eastern District. The expansion of the town initially put a strain on the bus network. Development of bus services in the town to accommodate these expansions are mentioned under the relevant chapters.

In terms of public transport in Northampton, the railways were first to arrive, doing so in 1845. At this time a branch line was opened from the London and Birmingham Railway. Connecting to the main line at Blisworth, the line ran through Northampton through to Peterborough. Known as the Northampton to Peterborough Railway, the line served Bridge Street Station, the first railway station in the town. A second station, Castle Station, opened on the site of the former Northampton Castle in 1859, providing a loop from the West Coast Main Line. A third station opened in 1872 called St John's Street Station. This was the northern terminus of the Midland Railway's branch line running between Northampton and Bedford. St John's Street station closed in 1939, with Bridge Street closing in 1964. This left Castle Station as the only station in Northampton and was subsequently renamed as Northampton Station.

Public transport was first introduced to Northampton in 1881 when a horse-drawn tram network operated by the Northampton Street Tramway Company commenced operation. In 1901, Northampton Borough Council took over the tram network, soon electrifying it. After this time, the Council used the name Northampton Corporation

Tramways for the operation. The Corporation was a late comer in operating motorbuses within Northampton, the first being introduced in 1923, with many independent bus operators providing motorbus operation into the town before this. Northampton Corporation Transport continued to expand within the Northampton area, restricted by the boundaries of the town.

F. & E. Beeden, the Midland Motor Bus Company Limited, the Northampton Motor Omnibus Co. Ltd, the Wellingborough Motor Omnibus Company and W.A. Nightingale & Sons were the pioneering motor bus operators in the Northampton area. Between them they provided a number of links to towns and villages outside of Northampton.

During early 1921, the directors of the Wellingborough Motor Omnibus Company Limited (WMOC) were looking at expanding the company into the Kettering and Northampton areas, with the view of establishing garages in these two areas. A contract was signed on 3 May 1921 for the construction of a garage facility on land purchased by the company in Houghton Road, Northampton. Northampton's other big operator, the United Counties Omnibus and Road Transport Company Limited (later United Counties Omnibus Company Ltd), was formed in September 1921, and they took over responsibility for the construction of the garage. This new operator was formed to take over the operations of the Wellingborough Motor Omnibus Company Limited. Two routes operating into Northampton were acquired from the latter Company, and as the 1920s and 1930s progressed, United Counties made significant inroads into Northampton, as well as Northamptonshire as a whole, acquiring a number of independents. United Counties became a strong operator in the Northampton area, and went through various owners, Tilling Group, National Bus Company and Stagecoach Holdings, the name being used until 2014 when the operators' licence was transferred to Midland Red South. However, under this new name, the Stagecoach Midlands operation in the town continues to be successful.

The County Borough of Northampton ceased to exist on the re-organisation of local government on 31 March 1974. After this date, Northampton Borough Council took over responsibilities. From 1 April, Northampton Corporation Transport became known as Northampton Borough Transport.

Alongside Northampton Corporation and United Counties, a number of independent operators provided services into Northampton, along with Midland Red and other larger operators. Some notable independent operators were York Brothers and Country Lion. The latter operator is still going strong in the Northampton area, operating school contracts, private hires, contract work and a few services in the town. Uno Buses of Hatfield, Hertfordshire started up an operation in conjunction with the University of Northampton in 2012 and has increased its presence in the town over the years, introducing a fleet of modern new buses.

As will be seen throughout the early part of this book, the early bus operators used the yards of a number of public houses or hotels to terminate their services, avoiding the need to obtain Hackney Carriage Licences. Those operators who did apply for these licences were allocated certain streets close to the town centre to terminate their services.

In addition to these, Northampton has had several bus stations. The first was located in Derngate and was mostly used by United Counties. This opened in October 1934 and served the town for many years before being replaced on 1 April 1976 by the infamous Greyfriars Bus Station. This gave Northampton its first central bus station, becoming the terminus of the majority of bus services operating into the town. Greyfriars, often referred to as an eyesore by many, was replaced by a new bus station in March 2014, given the name North Gate. It was located on the site of the former fish market. However, the new facility proved to be inadequate compared to Greyfriars. The smaller capacity of North Gate led to a number of services having to use The Drapery as their terminus and starting points.

This book explores the development of Northampton's tram and bus networks, looking at how the routes developed as demand grew. It also looks at how the local network of services was altered to incorporate the expansion of the town. Before we look at this, it is important that we briefly explore a couple of Acts of Parliament that affected the bus industry.

The Northampton Corporation Act was passed in 1922. Section 25 of this Act allowed Northampton Corporation Tramways to provide, maintain and operate motorbuses within the Borough boundaries of Northampton, along with roads outside the Borough provided consent was granted by the Minister of Transport and the local authority in which they wished to operate. This was, however, amended after opposition was met from United Counties. Following a meeting between the latter operator and the Deputy Town Clerk, it was amended so that Northampton Corporation Tramways could operate buses within 2¼ miles of Northampton Town Hall. Restrictions were also placed stating that they were not allowed to operate routes on roads where it was felt United Counties were already providing an efficient service.

Early bus services were governed by two Acts, the Town Police Clauses Acts of 1847 and 1889, and the Stage Carriage Act 1832. Under these Acts, early bus operators were required to obtain licences from the various local authorities in the areas where they wished to operate a service. In Northamptonshire, many of the local authorities of the time became responsible for this after passing byelaws. The Northampton Borough Council Watch Committee (NBCWC) governed the bus services operating into the town. This was mainly to protect the interests of the tramway. The NBCWC could set conditions on how much was charged for a fare in the areas where the trams operated. Both drivers and conductors were required to gain licences from each local authority that they operated into.

This was all changed by the passing of the Road Traffic Act 1930; this being passed on 1 August 1930. Under this new Act, responsibility for the licencing and granting of services in areas passed from local authorities to newly appointed Traffic Commissioners. The country was divided into different traffic areas. Northampton originally came under the East Midlands traffic area, remaining as such until 1990, when it transferred to the Eastern area. Bus and coach operators were required to apply for Road Service Licences under this new act which came into effect from 9 February 1931. Many services that had operated prior to this date were generally granted by the Traffic Commissioner. After this date vehicles were required to pass stringent tests and, if they passed, they were issued with a certificate of fitness. A single licence and badge was issued to drivers and conductors under this act, replacing the numerous local authority badges required prior to the Act.

David Beddall
Rushden, July 2023

1880–1909

1880

The Northampton Street Tramways Company was formed in January 1880. Soon after, parliamentary powers were obtained to build tramways on a number of roads within the town, these including Kettering Road, Wellingborough Road and Kingsthorpe Road.

1881

Just over a year passed before the first route opened. The service, commencing on 4 June, ran between West Bridge and the junction of Kettering Road/Kingsley Road. On 30 July, the route was extended from West Bridge to terminate at St James, Café Square, located between the junction of Weedon Road and Harlestone Road. A second route opened on 7 October 1881 between All Saints' Church, at the top end of the Drapery, and Barrack Avenue/St Georges Avenue, running along Kingsthorpe Road. A depot and stables were constructed at 72 Abington Street and were used to house the eight tramcars purchased for the services, these being pulled by a pair of horses.

1883–94

Further expansion took place from 4 January 1883, when the Kingsthorpe line was extended further into Kingsthorpe, running from Barrack Road/St Georges Avenue to a new terminus at Welford Road. The St James Café Square service was extended to the junction of Weedon Road and Melbourne Gardens, this later becoming Franklin Gardens. The introduction of the service saw two further tramcars purchased.

It took another ten years before the next tramway opened in Northampton. The line serving Wellingborough Road opened in May 1893. The service ran from Abington Square to the junction of Wellingborough Road and Roseholme Road. This expansion saw the doubling of the track in Abington Street, this location now being served by both the Kettering and Wellingborough Road services.

The original livery used by Northampton Street Tramways is unknown. However, different liveries were applied to the tramcars during 1893, depending on which service they were used on. Those on the Kingsley Park to Franklin Gardens service wore a green and white livery. Those used on the Wellingborough Road service wore a red and white livery, whilst the Kingsthorpe Road trams were blue and white.

It was planned that another tramway would be built between Gold Street and Bridge Street railway station. However, this idea was abandoned due to the steepness of Bridge Street itself, along with the difficulty of negotiating the level crossing of the railway. Demand grew for a service along this route, and on 5 April 1894 a horse-bus service commenced, linking All Saints' Church with St Mary's Church in Far Cotton, running via Bridge Street. Three single-deck horse-drawn buses were purchased for this service. These operated the service until 1907, when they were replaced by a pair of second-hand horse-drawn buses.

1901

The Tramways Act of 1870 gave local authorities the power to compulsorily purchase tramways that were operating within their areas after a twenty-one-year period. Under this law, the Tramways and Electric Light Committee of Northampton Borough Council took the decision to exercise this. An initial offer of £37,500 for the assets of 102 horses and twenty-two tramcars was offered to Northampton Street Tramways. This was refused, and a second offer of £38,700 was placed, this latter price being accepted. The new Company came into existence on 21 October 1901 and was named Northampton Corporation Tramways. Soon after the take-over, the decision was made to reconstruct, extend and electrify the system. This included new tramcar sheds, offices and a workshop. These new facilities were built in St James and replaced the Abington Street garage and stables. In total, the changes and electrification cost the Corporation £120,000. At this time, a number of trams were acquired, along with a pair of horse buses.

1904

Electrification of the Northampton tramway began in 1903 and was completed by the summer of 1904. At this time the fleet of horse-drawn tramcars were replaced by twenty electric tramcars. The St James-Kettering Road (Kingsley Park) and Wellingborough Road lines were the first to be converted, being finished by the date mentioned above. The Kingsthorpe line was opened shortly after, with electric trams taking over from horse-drawn ones on 19 August 1904.

A problem was encountered by the Corporation in Bridge Street, Far Cotton. At this location, the tram lines met the main railway line of the London & North Western Railway, who, until 1914, would not allow trams to pass over the rail lines. This meant that passengers had to alight the tram, cross the bridge and travel on a second tram which was pulled by a steam roller.

1910–1919

1910

The first passenger-carrying service between Northampton and Wellingborough commenced in 1910. William Valentine of Wellingborough had moved to the latter town in 1901, taking over the Wellingborough to Northampton carriers service of John Willis. This became a daily operation, and in 1909 Valentine motorised the service using an Argyll lorry, which he adapted to carry passengers.

1911

The name Frank Beeden will appear a number of times during this book, as Beeden was one of the pioneers in bus travel in the Northampton area. Beeden was a local sack merchant, who in 1911 purchased a Napier lorry which he also used to transport passengers for private hire parties, a practice he continued for a number of years.

1912

Thomas Henry Ernest Griffin of Daventry commenced business in August 1912. From this date, he was licensed to carry both goods and passengers. By 1914 he had commenced a daily service between Northampton, Campbell Square and Daventry, serving the villages of Flore, Weedon, Dodford, Newnham and Staverton.

As has already been seen in this chapter, local companies would convert a lorry for passenger use at this time. Albert Norman Heeps of Guilsborough was no different. Purchasing a lorry in 1912, a bus body was fitted to the vehicle when it was not in use as a lorry. This allowed Heeps to operate a service from Guilsborough, via Hollowell, Creaton, Spratton, Chapel Brampton to Northampton.

1913

A brief mention should be made here of Thomas Henry Clark of Rothwell. On 28 May 1913, he was granted a licence by Kettering Urban District Council. Clark did not operate a regular bus service, instead occasional excursions to both Kettering and the Bull Hotel in Northampton were operated.

Wellingborough Motor Omnibus Company Limited (WMOC) was formed on 3 May 1913. By June, the Company had established three services. One of these was a service between Wellingborough, Wilby, Earls Barton, Ecton and Northampton.

A new service connecting Northampton, Milton, Blisworth and Towcester was established by George Henry Clarke and George Dillow at some point between July and August 1913. The bus used was housed in the yard of the Plough Hotel, Northampton. However, this service was short-lived, ceasing in the autumn of 1913.

A second service began between Northampton and Earls Barton in September. Alfred Jackson, the landlord of the Stag, Earls Barton, purchased a charabanc in May and applied to the Northampton Borough Council Watch Committee for a Hackney Carriage Licence to stand a bus in Abingdon Square, Northampton. This new service operated on market days (Wednesdays and Saturdays).

Northampton-based funeral director Ann Bonham & Son purchased a pair of Lacre lorries in September. The original intention was to use these vehicles for furniture removals. Seats were fitted on occasions and the lorries were also used as charabancs.

In late 1913, Frank Beeden purchased a Napier covered charabanc. This charabanc, along with the fleet of lorries, operated from the yard of the Plough Hotel on Bridge Street. It was at this time that Beeden commenced his first local bus service, running between Northampton, Milton, Blisworth and Towcester.

1914

The name George Henry Clarke has already been mentioned above. In February 1914, he purchased a Maudslay double-decker. The following month, he applied to the Northampton Watch Committee to stand a bus in St Andrews Road, Northampton. From here, Clarke operated a service between Northampton and Daventry. By July 1914, competition was met on this route from the newly formed Northampton Motor Omnibus Company Ltd (NMOC). The latter company wasted no time introducing a service between Northampton, Weedon and Daventry, operating the service from St Andrews Road, Northampton.

Ann Bonham & Son applied for their first Hackney Carriage Licence in March. Bonham was granted permission to stand a charabanc at Regent Square, Northampton. Bonham continued to operate private hire work for a number of years.

Susan Elizabeth Hollowell, the proprietor of the Racehorse Inn located in Abington Square, Northampton, purchased a Maudslay Charabanc in April 1914. Hollowell applied for a Hackney Carriage Licence to stand a charabanc in Abington Square. This was granted and she commenced private hire work, continuing this until 1918 when the charabanc was sold at auction.

The first regular bus service between Northampton and Kettering was inaugurated by the WMOC on 5 June 1914, running via Broughton and Moulton Turn on a daily basis. A low rail bridge on Northampton Road, Kettering meant that the route was operated by single-decks.

The WMOC met opposition from the Northampton Tramways Committee during 1914 about the operation of services into Northampton along both Wellingborough and Kettering roads. It was suggested that passengers should transfer onto trams at the relevant termini on these roads. It was also suggested that transfer tickets would be issued from the buses to the trams. Despite this, the WMOC were granted permission to stand vehicles in Abington Square, Northampton.

A carriers' service between West Haddon and Northampton, Cross Keys had been established by Alfred Looker of West Haddon, this operating on a Wednesday and Saturday. In July, a Maudslay van was purchased, being licensed by Looker to carry both goods and passengers between the two locations. This continued for many years.

Wappenham-based Frederick George Archer commenced a service between the Lord Palmerston public house in Northampton and the villages of Abethorpe and Wappenham, this also operating on Wednesdays and Saturdays. Like Looker, a van was purchased and fitted with seats.

George Watson of Moulton was an established carrier between the village and nearby Northampton. He replaced his horse and cart with a Daimler van in 1914. Watson used this van to operate a daily service between Moulton and Northampton, providing three journeys a day. This service ceased during 1916.

During the First World War, Frank Beeden experimented with the use of town gas to power his fleet of buses, being joined by the Midland Motor Bus Co. Ltd. In the case of Beeden, the gas bags were produced by Barton Bros. of Beeston, Nottinghamshire, Beeden later becoming a merchant for Barton Bros. products. These were the only two operators in Northamptonshire to experiment with this type of fuel at this time.

The horse-bus operation between All Saints' Church and Far Cotton, introduced by the Northampton Street Tramways Company and later operated by Northampton Corporation Tramways, came to an end on 23 October 1914, lasting just over twenty years. The service was replaced by an extension of the tramway to Far Cotton from this date, seeing seven extra tramcars taken into stock.

1915

William Checkley of The Firs, Brixworth commenced operation of a Wednesday and Saturday service between Brixworth and Northampton. The service originally terminated in the yard of the Crosskeys public house in Sheep Street. Checkley was granted a Hackney Carriage Licence in May 1915, after which time he was granted permission to use Regent Square as a terminus.

The Northampton Motor Omnibus Co. Ltd started a second service on 1 August 1915. Starting at Guildhall Road, Northampton, the route served Brafield, Denton, Castle Ashby, Yardley Hastings, Lavendon, Turvey and Bromham before terminating at St Peters Green, Bedford. Later in the year, on 16 October, a third service was started by the Northampton Motor Omnibus Co. Ltd. It linked Northampton with Harlestone, East Haddon and Long Buckby. On 10 November, a fourth service was added. It ran between Northampton, Roade, Stoke Bruerne, Grafton Regis, Yardley Gobion, Potterspury and Old Stratford. Both services ran on Wednesdays, Saturdays and Sundays.

F&E Beeden encountered competition on its Northampton to Towcester service in December 1915 when the Midland Motor Bus Company Limited commenced operation of a service between Northampton, Guildhall Road and Silverstone, running through the villages of Milton, Blisworth, Towcester and Whittlebury.

On 6 December 1915, George Henry Clarke sold his Maudslay double-deck to the newly formed Midland Motor Bus Company, of which he became one of the directors.

In late 1915 the Midland Motor Bus Company Limited of Northampton commenced operation of a service between St Andrews Road, Northampton and Daventry. The route also served Kislingbury Turn, Harpole Turn, Flore, Weedon, Dodford Turn and Newnham Turn. The Northampton Motor Omnibus Company Limited and George Henry Clarke were both already providing a service over this route. The Midland Motor Bus Co. Ltd and Northampton Motor Omnibus Co. Ltd both later operated a joint timetable between Northampton and Daventry. The timings of Clarke's Northampton to Daventry route were taken over by Midland in 1915. On 8 November, Midland commenced operation of their second service. This again started in St Andrews Road, Northampton and travelled through the villages of Harlestone, West Haddon, Crick and Hillmorton before reaching its final destination at Barby Road, Rugby. Before the close of 1915, the Midland Motor Bus Company established a third service from Northampton. Starting from Guildhall Road, Northampton, this service ran out to Silverstone, servicing the villages of Milton, Blisworth, Towcester and Whittlebury on its way. The service commenced on 15 December 1915 and ran in competition with F&E Beeden. At the same time, a service commenced between Northampton, Kislingbury, Bugbrooke and Nether Heyford.

The Wellingborough Motor Omnibus Company Limited reduced the frequency of the Wellingborough to Northampton service during the First World War. The change was brought about by restrictions on petrol supplies, along with a shortage of labour. At an unknown date during the war, the Kettering to Northampton service was withdrawn.

1916

The Midland Motor Omnibus Co. Ltd officially became a limited company on 29 January 1916. The registered office was at 9 George Row, Northampton, with a garage at Bedford Place, just off Derngate. Midland commenced operation of a service between Northampton, Stoke Goldington and Newport Pagnell. It is unclear when exactly this service started but it is thought to have started at some point during 1916. In March, the Northampton, West Haddon, Rugby and Coventry service was diverted to serve Kilsby and Hillmorton. After a short period of operation, this service was withdrawn in January 1916. After Midland's withdrawal from this service, the Northampton Motor Omnibus Company extended their Northampton to Long Buckby service to West Haddon.

On 28 June 1916, the Northampton Motor Omnibus Co. Ltd introduced a short service between St Andrews Road, Northampton and Duston Military Hospital on a Wednesday and Saturday. Around the same time, a former London B-type was used to convey the wounded between Northampton Castle Station and Berrywood Hospital in Duston. The introduction of petrol restrictions saw the local services of the Northampton Motor Omnibus Co. Ltd cut on Tuesdays and Fridays. The Company joined forces with the Midland Bus Company and jointly operated the Northampton, Weedon and Daventry service. Towards the end of 1916, the Northampton to Long Buckby service was extended to West Haddon.

1917

Northampton Borough Council Watch Committee granted Walter William Webster of Guilsborough a Hackney Carriage Licence on 10 September, to ply for hire from Regent Square, Northampton. For a short period of time after this date, Webster provided a service between Guilsborough and Northampton.

The Northampton to Bedford service of the Northampton Motor Omnibus Co. Ltd was curtailed to Lavendon on 1 November 1917.

1918

The Northampton to Brixworth service operated by William Checkley of Brixworth ceased operation during 1918.

1919

On 1 May 1919, the Wellingborough Motor Omnibus Company Limited reintroduced its Kettering to Northampton service which had been withdrawn during the war period.

F&E Beeden applied in May 1919 to Northamptonshire County Council to operate a service between the Northampton Plough Hotel and Newport Pagnell. Permission was granted and the service commenced shortly after. It ran via Hardingstone, Piddington, Hackleton, Horton, Stoke Goldington, Gayhurst and Lathbury. Short workings were also operated between Northampton, Hardingstone and Piddington. The route was set up in competition with a similar service operated by the Midland Motor Bus Company.

At the same time, Beeden introduced a Saturday only extension on the Northampton to Towcester service, running past the latter destination to serve the villages of Abthorpe and Wappenham. In addition, a Wednesday, Saturday and Sunday operation was introduced between the Plough Hotel and Whittlebury, travelling through Milton, Blisworth, Shutlanger and Paulerspury on its journey.

May 1919 also saw John Willis of Earls Barton apply to the Northampton Borough Council Watch Committee for a Hackney Carriage licence. Two months later it was granted, allowing Willis to ply for hire from Campbell Square, Northampton on Wednesdays and Saturdays. Soon after, he commenced a service between Wellingborough, Wilby, Earls Barton, Ecton, Weston Favell and Northampton, on the days previously mentioned. However, competition from the Wellingborough Motor Omnibus Co. Ltd led to the withdrawal of the service. Willis went on to operate a taxi business.

During October 1919, the Leather Fair was being held at the Agricultural Hall in London. For this the Northampton Motor Omnibus Co. Ltd operated a daily service to the event from Northampton for the week. Before 1919 came to a close, the Northampton Motor Omnibus Co. Ltd had a threat of competition from the National Steam Car Co. Ltd. National, based in Bedford, made applications to the Northampton Borough Council Watch Committee in 1919 for permission to operate services from Northampton to Daventry, Long Buckby, Towcester and Stony Stratford using sixteen omnibuses. National were met with objections from the Northampton Motor Omnibus Co. Ltd, along with the Midland Motor Bus Co. and F&E Beeden all voicing concerns and attended a meeting on 2 December 1919. As a result, the Watch Committee deferred the decision to grant licences for these services. Alongside these applications, National had also made an application to operate a service between Bedford and Northampton. A temporary licence was issued for the latter company to operate two buses between the two destinations, the service commencing in October 1919. It was not until June 1920 that a final decision was made. The Watch Committee upheld its decision to only grant National a licence for the Bedford service, this becoming a permanent route from this time.

In 1919, George Leonard Edwards commenced a bus service from Paulerspury, located 3 miles south-east of Towcester, running north to Northampton. The route called at Alderton, Stoke Bruerne, Roade and Wootton en route. The Northampton terminus was located on waste ground between Bridge Street and Cattle Market Road. The service ran on Wednesdays, Saturdays and Sundays, operating unchanged over its thirty-three-year history.

George Keeber of Wellingborough never operated stage-carriage services. However, in 1919 he applied to Northampton Borough Council for a motor lorry to set down and pick up passengers from outside St Edmunds Church on Wellingborough Road, Northampton. However, the services were intermittent and only operated on special occasions.

Brothers Albert and Charles Branson of Spratton purchased a former military lorry which was fitted with wooden seats in 1919 and used it on a service between Spratton and Northampton. Operating successfully for over a year, the service ceased after competitors offered the public better vehicles to travel on.

During the mid-nineteenth century, Phoebe Smart began a carrier's service between Greens Norton and Northampton, the service ceasing after her death. In 1919, her grandson, Arthur Basford, re-commenced this service, running via Towcester and terminating in the yard of the Woolpack Inn, Bridge Street, Northampton. Like a number of similar services at this time, it operated on Wednesdays and Saturdays, and a horse and cart was used. In December 1919, Basford purchased a Model T Ford lorry to which he fitted an enclosed body. Inside he fitted wooden forms. This Ford allowed Basford to operate a bus service from Greens Norton to Northampton, Woolpack Inn, serving Towcester and Blisworth on the way. However, this Ford T was very underpowered and not suitable for the hilly service, especially when fully loaded. A couple of years later, the Ford was replaced by a Daimler vehicle, this also being converted from a lorry. On other days, Basford operated a number of private hires.

In 1919, Samuel Walter Kirton of Eastcote commenced a carrier's service between Astcote, Eastcote, Rothersthorpe and the Bull and Butcher in Bridge Street, Northampton. Using a horse and cart, passengers were soon carried on this Wednesday and Saturday service.

At an unknown date after the First World War, Midland Motor Bus Co. Ltd extended its Northampton, Towcester and Silverstone service to Brackley.

Welford-based Thomas Miller Senior was known in his village for being a carrier, operating into Northampton on Wednesday and Saturdays. In 1919 his son, Thomas James, joined the business and soon after a Napier lorry was purchased which was licensed as a public conveyance.

Just after the First World War ended, in 1919 Samuel Walters of Helmdon started a bus service between Greatworth and the Cross Keys on Sheep Street, Northampton. The service operated on a Wednesday, Saturday and Sunday. It served the villages of Culworth, Sulgrave, Helmdon, Wappenham, Abthorpe, Towcester, Blisworth and Milton.

Between 1919 and 1921, F&E Beeden continued to expand the private hire part of his business.

1920–1929

1920

The Northampton Motor Omnibus Company increased the frequency on their Northampton to Lavendon service in April 1920, with some journeys being extended to Bozeat from this time. The company introduced a fifth route from 21 August, operating between Northampton and Market Harborough, via Pitsford, Brixworth, Lamport, Maidwell, Kelmarsh and Great Oxendon.

The Wellingborough Motor Omnibus Company received complaints from local traders regarding mud splashes on Wellingborough Road, some of these dating back to 1914. Further complaints were received in June 1920, and to help combat this the Northampton Watch Committee changed the WMOC's termini from September 1920. The Kettering service had a new terminus at the junction of Kettering Road and Hood Street; whilst the Wellingborough service was rerouted via Abington Avenue, terminating at the junction with Kettering Road.

Thomas Miller and Sons commenced a service in the early 1920s between Northampton and Welford. The route also served the villages of Cold Ashby, Thornby, Creaton, Spratton and Chapel Brampton. The route was operated by a lorry which carried a purpose-built bus body.

A Northampton based haulage contractor trading under the name of Clarke purchased a charabanc in 1920. Over the course of July and August a number of excursions were operated. After the 1920 season, no further trace can be found of this operator. F.R. Harris had a motor and engineering business on the Old Towcester Road in Northampton. By August 1920 he had acquired a twelve-seat Austin charabanc and advertised this for hire. The only known private hire operated by Harris was one from his garage in Northampton to Towcester Races in 1921.

George William Langley of Ecton purchased a Ford T in September 1920, licencing it to transport both goods and passengers. Langley used this vehicle to convey passengers between Ecton and Northampton on Wednesdays and Saturdays. The service ran for no more than two years, an exact date of the cessation not being known.

September also saw a service commence between Finedon, Wellingborough and Northampton. The route was operated by Herbert Samuel Stanley and John William Trevor of Finedon, who had applied to the Wellingborough Urban District Council after purchasing a bus.

David Nicholson of Rushden inaugurated a service between Irthlingborough, Wellingborough and Northampton in 1920. In November, Nicholson became part of the team who formed the Progressive Motor Omnibus Services (Wellingborough) Ltd. The company was granted a licence in February 1921 to operate a service between Wellingborough, Wilby, Earls Barton and Northampton, the bus terminating in Sheep Street.

Charles Robert Bradley of Great Everdon purchased a Napier vehicle for the use of transporting the public. Little is known about his operation, but it is thought that Bradley operated a market day service between Everdon and Northampton. The introduction of a service between the two locations by the Northampton Motor Omnibus Co. in 1921 is thought to have seen this service cease operation.

Alfred Jackson applied to the Northampton Watch Committee in 1920 to move his Northampton terminus from Abington Square to Abington Park Gates, this being done so it was closer to Northampton Town Football Club's ground. Exact dates for a service operated by Ramsford Humphrey of Old Stratford between Collingtree and Northampton are unknown. However, it is known that it operated at some point in the early 1920s.

Robert Leathersich of Walgrave commenced a service in 1920 between Walgrave and Northampton using an old lorry fitted with a covered body and seats. The route also served Hannington, Holcot and Moulton, terminating in the yard of the Stag's Head on Abington Street.

Thomas Frederick Reeve of Pattishall had an established carrier service dating from just after the First World War. He inaugurated a bus service between Grimscote, Cold Higham, Fosters Booth, Pattishall, Astcote, Eastcote, Dalscote, Rothersthorpe and the Plough Hotel, Northampton in 1920. This operated on Wednesdays and Saturdays only.

Another name to add to the private hire and excursion operators in the Northampton area was Henry Thomas Woolley. He commenced operating these using charabancs in 1920, although his licence was not officially granted until March 1921. From this date, he was granted permission to use either Market Square, Regent Square or Campbell Square as departure points.

Little is known about the operation of William Thomas Ponton of Walgrave. It is, however, known that this proprietor operated a service between Scaldwell, Brixworth and the Bull Hotel, Regent Square, Northampton. However, the service had ceased by the time the 1930 Road Traffic Act came into force.

1921

The WMOC and Progressive Motor Omnibus Services Limited were both granted permission to stand buses in Abington Street, close to the new theatre, in April 1921. However, the Progressive company withdrew its services in the Northampton area soon after and it is unknown if these arrangements were carried out. The WMOC were also allowed to return to their stand in Abington Square soon after.

An application was made by William Alfred Nightingale in late 1920 to run a service between Towcester, Wheatsheaf Hotel, Blisworth, Milton and Northampton, St Johns Street. The route ran in competition with F&E Beeden and the Midland Motor Bus Company, operating on Wednesdays, Thursdays, Saturdays and Sundays. Over the coming years, the Nightingale fleet grew, moving towards excursions and private hire work.

William Edward Coombs was another operator to use charabancs on tours and private hire work. These commenced from February 1921, using the Queen's Arms on Kettering Road, Northampton as a departure point. An application was made to the Northampton Watch Committee in April to stand two charabancs on Northampton Market Square, Regent Square being used on Wednesdays and Saturdays.

Arthur Edwin Hopkins and John Wilfred Howells of Wellingborough formed a partnership in 1921, applying to the Northampton Watch Committee in June to set down and pick up passengers from St Edmunds Church on Wellingborough Road, this being granted. The service between Northampton and Wellingborough operated until 1923 when the partnership was dissolved.

Few details are known about the operations of H.W. Broughton & C.F. Brown of Creaton. However, the pair applied to ply for hire from Regent Square or Campbell Square, Northampton. It is believed that they operated a service between Northampton and Creaton from June 1921 until March 1922.

The NMOC service between Northampton and Market Harborough was cut back to terminate at Brixworth in June 1921. The National Steam Car Co. of Bedford discontinued their service between Northampton and Bedford in July 1921, it being curtailed at Lavendon. The NMOC took passengers from Lavendon to Northampton. A sixth route was introduced by the NMOC on 5 October, running between Northampton, Chapel Brampton, Spratton, Creaton, Hollowell, Guilsborough, Thornby and Welford. The service operated on Wednesdays, Saturdays and Sundays. Soon after, another route was introduced between Northampton, Kislingbury, Bugbrooke, Lower Heyford, Lower and Upper Weedon, Everdon, Newnham and Badby.

Harbert Phillips of Long Buckby purchased a Ford T bus in June, which he initially used on private hire work. However, later in the year he commenced a Saturday-only service between Long Buckby and St Andrews Road, Northampton. The service also called at East Haddon, Harlestone and Duston. A Wednesday and Sunday service was introduced from an unknown date.

The final route development for June 1921 saw William Valentine of Wellingborough apply to set down and pick up passengers from the Wellingborough Road tram terminus. This was granted and was operated until 1922.

The United Counties Omnibus and Road Transport Co. Limited was formed on 1 September 1921, taking over the operations of the Wellingborough Motor Omnibus Company Limited. Two services were operating into Northampton at the time of takeover: the 2 (Irthlingborough-Finedon-Wellingborough-Wilby-Earls Barton-Ecton-Northampton) and the 6 (Kettering-Broughton-Moulton Turn-Northampton). 16 September saw United Counties enter into a contract with the Progressive Motor Omnibus Services (Wellingborough) Ltd not to establish routes in competition in the Northampton area. Soon after the agreement was signed, Progressive moved its operations to Lincolnshire.

In November 1921, Jack Botterill and Arthur Houghton applied to the Watch Committee to operate a service from St Andrews Road, Northampton to Bugbrooke Wharf, via Bugbrooke Village and Kislingbury. This was granted and the route ran on weekends. William Charles Nutt of Harpole also applied to run from the same terminus in Northampton. Again, this was granted, and Nutt operated a service between Northampton and Harpole, via Upton and the A45, commencing on 18 November.

George Richardson of Hartwell applied to the Watch Committee in December 1921 to operate a service from the Plough Hotel in Bridge Street, Northampton to Wootton, Quinton and Hartwell. This was granted, and the service was soon extended to Hanslope. From an unknown date, a second service was introduced between Hartwell, Ashton, Roade, Courteenhall Turn, Collingtree Turn, Wootton and Northampton, a route that already had a number of operators. The company traded as Hartwell Motor Services.

In 1921, Arthur Bird obtained a licence to operate excursions from Northampton Market Square. He was joined by Elizabeth Ann Tomkins of Cotton End, Northampton, who also commenced operating excursions from Northampton in 1921.

Surridge Bros. (Alfred and Reginald Surridge) were granted a Hackney Carriage Licence to stand a bus in St Andrews Road, Northampton. From here they operated a service to Harpole via Upton and the A45.

Alfred Ernest Walmsley of Northampton commenced operation of a local service in 1921 between the Shakespeare Inn, Marefair, Northampton and the Squirrels Public House, Duston, this soon being extended to Berrywood Gates. Capital for the service was provided by Mrs Violet Andrews.

1922

The landlord of the Shakespeare Inn, Marefair (mentioned above), Charlie Billington, commenced operation of a service between there and New Duston, Berrywood Gates or the Rifle Butt, in January 1922. Certain journeys were extended to nearby Harlestone. Later in the year, Billington commenced operation of excursions and tours from Northampton Market Square.

January also saw Andrew Law & Son of Brafield apply to the Watch Committee to pick up and set down passengers from Derngate, Northampton. This was duly granted in February and a service between Grendon, Castle Ashby, Whiston, Cogenhoe, Brafield, Little and Great Houghton and Northampton soon commenced. A stop was also served at the Black Boy Hotel on Dychurch Lane.

In February, William Henry Swann of Greens Norton purchased a Star vehicle. With this, he commenced a service linking Greens Norton, Towcester, Blisworth, Milton Malsor and Northampton, terminating at the Woolpack Inn, Bridge Street. The service ran for a couple of years before ceasing.

Henry Thomas Woolley was a name associated with tours and excursions from Northampton. From 8 March, he commenced a Wednesday and Saturday service between Campbell Square, Northampton and Moulton, Holcot and Walgrave. This was a route already operated by the Leathersich brothers. 22 October saw the service extended to Old, becoming a daily service.

Elizabeth Tomkins had been operating excursions from Northampton since 1921. In 1922 she officially applied to the Watch Committee to ply for hire from Northampton Market Square. From December, she applied to operate a bus from St John's Street, Northampton which was granted. This allowed Tomkins to continue to officially operate a daily service between Northampton and Cosgrove, having unofficially operated one since August.

Frederick Whitlock of Towcester also applied for a licence to operate from St John's Street. The licence was granted in June, after which time Whitlock began operating a Wednesday, Saturday and Sunday service between Greens Norton, Towcester, Blisworth, Milton and Northampton.

The partnership between Violet Andrews and Alfred Walmsley ended in 1922 after a disagreement. After this, Walmsley continued operating his service from Horseshoe Street, Northampton travelling out to Duston. Mrs Andrews then used the vehicle for private hire work, purchasing a second to operate a service between Northampton and The Squirrels and Berrywood Gates, Duston. Known as the Violet service, the route became successful whilst the one operated by Walmsley was not, and it soon ceased operation.

Samuel Kirton of Eastcote established a carrier's service between Ascote and Northampton in 1919. In July 1922, he purchased a Ford T and continued the service, diverting it into Gayton and Milton. This provided Gayton with its first bus service.

Albert Owen Clarke and Joseph Dilley formed a partnership in 1922 and started a bus service between Moulton and Northampton. Applying to the Watch Committee in May, the service soon started.

The National Omnibus Company Limited made an application to the Watch Committee for eleven Hackney Carriage licences in May 1922 for a service between Newport Pagnell and Northampton. The application was withdrawn as F.E. Beeden and the Midland Motor Bus Company were both operating over this route.

G.S. Bird of St James, Northampton, was granted a Hackney Carriage Licence from 11 September 1922 to operate a charabanc from Northampton Market Square. The licence expired on 25 March 1923, after which time no further applications were made.

Arthur Bird applied for a licence to operate a service between Northampton, Weston Underwood, Stoke Goldington, Hackleton and Olney from October 1922. This was granted with the Northampton terminus being at St Johns Street.

The Midland Motor Bus Co. Ltd ceased operation of its Northampton to Daventry service from October 1922, making the Northampton Motor Omnibus Co. the sole operator on this service.

In 1922, Kingston Bros. of Woodend purchased a Lancia single-decker, with which they started a Wednesday, Saturday and Sunday only service between Woodend and the Plough Hotel, Bridge Street. It served the villages of Blakesley, Adstone, Maidford, Litchborough, Bugbrooke and Kislingbury.

Arthur Houghton commenced a service between Fosters Booth, Bugbrooke, Kislingbury and Northampton in 1922. The route lasted until 1924.

Silverstone-based Sydney Charles Kingston purchased a former First World War ambulance which he converted to a bus. He used the vehicle on a service between Silverstone and Northampton Cattle Market, also serving Towcester and Blisworth. The route was later extended from Silverstone to Syresham. Kingston applied to stand a bus on Market Square from where he would operate tours. This was refused.

William Nutt of Harpole commenced operation of a second service in 1922. The Saturday only service ran between Great Brington, Little Brington, Nobottle, Old Duston and Northampton. Around the same time a third service was introduced, running between Little Brington and Northampton via Great Brington, Upper Harlestone and New Duston.

Cobbler William Ainge applied in May to the Watch Committee to ply for hire using a charabanc from Guildhall Road. He wished to operate a service from this location to the Berrywood area of Old Duston. He also applied for an excursion licence from Northampton Market Square. These were both granted from 15 May.

Allchin is a name synonymous with road transport in the Northampton area, with the long-distance and coach holiday business, along with the construction of steam road vehicles. 1920 saw Allchin establish a haulage business, gaining a contract with the British United Machinery Company of Leicester. During the holiday period, he attached a bus body to a lorry and used it on excursions. In 1922, Allchin purchased two ambulances which he fitted with charabanc bodies and in the summer of 1922 he applied to the Watch Committee to operate tours and excursions from Market Square, Northampton, with Regent Square being added as a terminus on Wednesdays and Saturdays.

1923

In April 1923, John William Buckseall & Son applied to the Watch Committee for a Hackney Carriage Licence. This was granted and Buckseall operated a service between Northampton and Upper Weedon. He became another short-lived operator, ceasing operation on 25 March 1924.

Coombs & Sons made another application to the Watch Committee in June 1923 to move the stand for the vehicles to Derngate. This was done to benefit the new service between Northampton, Rothersthorpe, Dalscote, Eastcote, Astcote, Pattishall, Fosters Booth, Cold Higham, Grimscote, Litchborough, Maidford, Adstone, Canons Ashby and Moreton Pinkney.

Maurice Henry Spreuls of Scaldwell purchased a Reo bus in September. He used the vehicle to start a service between Northampton and Old, running via Scaldwell, Brixworth, Pitsford Turn and Boughton Turn. Operating on Wednesdays, Saturdays and Sundays, the route terminated in the yard of a public house on Sheep Street.

A brief partnership was made between Charlie Billington and William Thomas Benson in 1923, when the Shakespeare Omnibus Company was formed. Billington continued the operation of this Company upon the dissolution of the partnership in November 1923. Benson went on to form the Squirrels Bus Service of Old Duston in November, partnering with his son. This new operator provided a service between Old Duston and St Andrews Road, Northampton.

A second licence was applied for by Clarke and Dilley to operate a service between Moulton and Northampton, mentioned under the 1922 heading. They applied to stand a bus in Campbell Square, Northampton.

F.E. Beeden introduced route numbers to their services in 1923. The Towcester route became route 4; the Newport Pagnell service the 1. Route 2 was allocated to the Wappenham service, whilst the Whittlebury service took route number 3. W.A. Nightingale competed with Beeden on the Towcester service, whilst Wesley's of Stoke Goldington competed with Beeden on the Newport Pagnell to Stoke Goldington section of route 1.

Thomas George Lamb used an Austin car in 1923 to convey passengers from Byfield and the surrounding areas to Northampton. The service was a success and a purpose-built bus was purchased for the route in 1927.

Jabez Minney of Yardley Hastings operated a carrier's service between the village and Northampton on market days, having a capacity for eight passengers. In 1923, he purchased a Chevrolet bus, starting a service from Yardley Hastings to the Black Boy Inn on Dychurch Lane, Northampton. The route served Denton, Brafield and the Houghtons. Houghton Road, Derngate, Hazelwood Road, St Giles Street and Fish Street were used to access Northampton.

Pattishall-based Thomas Reeve, who operated a Grimscote to Northampton service, was declared bankrupt in 1923. His son, Bernard Reeve, paid his father's debts and took over the business. He continued the service, adding a Sunday service.

Herbert Stanley continued operating his service between Finedon, Wellingborough and Northampton after his partnership with John Trevor ceased in 1923. He ceased operation of this service in 1924 after competition was met from United Counties.

Northampton Corporation Tramways introduced their first motorbuses on two services in 1923. The route was numbered 1 and ran between St James, Kingsthorpe and Abington, terminating at the junction of Abington Avenue and Park Avenue North. Route 2 operated between Northampton town centre, Abington Park and Briton Road. Both services commenced on 13 September. The St James garage was extended to accommodate these vehicles.

1924

The Midland Motor Bus Co. Ltd entered voluntary liquidation in February 1924, from which time their services to Northampton ceased.

Harry and George Albert Clarke, sons of George Henry Clark, a name already mentioned in this book, applied to the Northampton Watch Committee in 1924 to stand a single bus in St Andrews Road, Northampton. This was granted from 14 June, at which time a service commenced operation between Northampton and Lower Weedon. The service ran via Kislingbury, Lower Heyford, Flore and Weedon.

June saw Charles Henry Sheffield apply to the Watch Committee for a licence to operate a service between Northampton, Overstone, Sywell, Mears Ashby, Wilby and Wellingborough. The service operated on Wednesdays and Saturdays. The service became popular, seeing a daily service introduced. Sheffield used the name Progressive Bus Service, the service lasting until 1927. Sheffield previously operated excursions and tours from Northampton Market Square.

An application was received by the Watch Committee from Alfred Turner of Milton Malsor in the summer of 1924. He wished to operate a service between Milton Malsor and Northampton. The licence was, however, refused, as it was felt that there was a good level of service on this route already. This did not deter Turner, who soon started a service between Gayton, Milton Malsor and the Plough Hotel, Northampton. The latter location was private property, meaning Turner did not need a Hackney Carriage Licence.

William Jackson of Earls Barton applied to operate from Regents Square, Northampton whilst operating a service to Brixworth in September 1924. This was another application that was refused by the Council on the same basis that the level of service being provided already was adequate. The service was operated, terminating in the yard of a public house in Sheep Street. He was granted a licence in 1925.

In November 1924, John Mills of Brixworth, who traded as Maroon Bus Service, commenced operation between Brixworth and Northampton, Cross Keys. Mills had previously operated a carrier's service over a similar route.

The name York Brothers of Cogenhoe is one that is synonymous with the Northamptonshire area bus industry. The name came about in November 1924 when a freight service between Cogenhoe and Northampton was established on Wednesdays and Saturdays. A year later, a passenger service was established.

The partnership between Clarke and Dilley was dissolved in this year, although Clarke continued to operate their Northampton to Moulton service, introduced by the pair in 1922.

The Violet, operated by Violet Andrews, was acquired by Alfred Wharmsley during 1924. Wharmsley moved the Northampton terminus to the Grand Hotel on Gold Street, bringing the terminus closer to Northampton town centre. The Shakespeare Bus Company was also competing over the route between Northampton and Duston at this time.

A private hire coach business was set up by Hardwick and Mann from the Moore Street garage in the Kingsley area of the town. Joseph Mann was granted a Hackney Carriage Licence to ply for hire from both Northampton Market Square and Campbell Square, the latter being used on market days. However, the operation did not last long, being purchased by Allchin and Sons in February 1926.

Albert Norman Heeps sold his Northampton to Guilsborough service to John 'Jack' Smith, one of his drivers. He established a base in Creaton and applied for a Hackney

Carriage Licence to operate a charabanc from Campbell Square and Regent Square, Northampton to Creaton, via Spratton and Chapel Brampton. Trading as the Blue Fly Bus Service, the route operated Wednesdays and Saturdays.

Spring 1924 saw the opening of the British Empire Exhibition at Wembley Park, London. Nightingale & Sons commenced a daily coach service between Northampton and the exhibition, joined shortly after by Allchin & Sons who introduced a Thursday and Saturday only express service, this later also becoming a daily one.

At the same time, Allchin was also offering five-day excursions to a number of UK locations including Wales and the Cheddar Gorge and Caves. Allchin also offered day tours to the Peak District and Stratford-on-Avon amongst some destinations served. A new summer seaside service was introduced to Bournemouth, running in August and September.

Northampton Corporation applied to the Minister of Transport to extend route 2 from Briton Road to Weston Favell. Objections were met from both Northamptonshire County Council and United Counties. The County Council's objections were about the turning of buses in Trumpet Lane, at the junction of Wellingborough Road, which, in the Council's view, would affect the flow of traffic using the latter road. United Counties' objection was that the extension of the service would exceed the 2¼ mile restriction.

1925

Walkers Transport Services was a well-known goods operator in Northamptonshire. In October 1924, owner Arthur Walker applied to the Watch Committee for a Hackney Carriage Licence; this being refused. He applied a second time and it was granted in February 1925. Under the name Sunshine, he operated excursions and tours from Campbell Square or Market Square.

Knight was another name that became associated with the transport industry in Northamptonshire. In March 1925, Sarah Jane Knight and her husband Charles inaugurated a service from Denton and Brafield to Northampton, again on Wednesdays and Saturdays. It was soon extended eastwards to Yardley Hastings, Olney, Lavendon and Harrold. This ran in competition with Northampton Motor Omnibus Co. Ltd's service between Northampton, Harrold and Bozeat and Agnes Minney's Northampton to Yardley Hastings service; as well as Law & Son's Brafield to Northampton service. The service traded under the Sally Omnibus Service name.

Joseph Charles Abram of Station Road, Earls Barton commenced operation of a service between Wellingborough, Market Square and Northampton, Campbell Square in February, this being a single-journey service. It officially started on 25 May 1925, operating Mondays to Saturdays. This was, however, short lived. It became a Saturday only service for Northampton Town Football Club, running between September and April.

In April 1925, George Blundell of Spratton began a service between Spratton, Chapel Brampton and Northampton. This Wednesday and Saturday only service terminated at the Bull Hotel located on Regent Square.

A month later, in May, Arthur Cowley applied to the Watch Committee for a Hackney Carriage Licence to operate a service between Campbell Square, Northampton to Mears Ashby, serving Overstone and Sywell. A fatal accident on the route led Cowley to give up the service later in the year.

A Wednesday and Saturday only service was started by York Bros. in 1925, operating between Cogenhoe, Little Billing and Northampton, terminating at the Black Boy Hotel. Demand grew for the service, leading to it becoming a daily operation, with the exception of Sundays.

George Tomlin, based in Wootton, purchased a Chevrolet bus in June 1925. He used this vehicle on a service between Wootton, Hardingstone and the Knightley Arms located on Commercial Street, Northampton.

The 1925 summer season again saw Allchin operate a range of holidays and tours, these expanded to serve Devon, the Lake District, Scotland and Wales. Alongside these the seaside specials continued.

On 9 September, Wilfred Gibson of Hardingstone commenced a bus service between Walgrave and Northampton. The route also served the villages of Hannington, Holcot and Moulton. The service ran in direct competition with Leathersich Bros. It was later extended to Old. From 19 October, Gibson gained a licence to operate the service from Campbell Square. Also, from an unknown date in the late 1920s, Gibson gained a contract for a lunchtime workers service from the Sears Shoe Factory in Northampton.

George Keeber of Wellingborough made an application to the Watch Committee in October 1925 to operate a bus from Campbell Square. Keeber had been operating a service between Wellingborough and Northampton since 1919, terminating at St Edmund's Church on Wellingborough Road.

Frederick Collins was an established coal merchant and carrier based in Moreton Pinkney, operating a carrier's service to Northampton on Saturdays. In 1925, he purchased a Ford T and continued the service, although it had ceased by the introduction of the Road Traffic Act 1930.

Andrew Law of Brafield approached Charles Knight of Denton about introducing a worker's bus from the village to Northampton. The latter operator had no intention of operating such a service, so Law introduced a peak time route between Denton, Brafield and Northampton.

A service between The Garage, Fosters Booth and the Plough Hotel was established by Mr Parkinson Barnes in 1925. It also served Pattishall, Astcote, Eastcote, Dalscote and Rothersthorpe. The service operated until 1927.

Henry Chinn of Towcester was granted a Hackney Carriage Licence to operate a service from Derngate or Cattle Market Road, Blisworth, Shutlanger, Heathencote, Paulerspury, Pury End, the A5 and Towcester.

Amy Ayres and Wallace Gaffield established a private hire business after purchasing a second-hand bus in 1925. The couple operated out of a base at Plevna Cottage in Hardingstone, just outside of Northampton.

The terminus of the Northampton local services operated by F.E. Beeden moved from the Plough Hotel to bus stands in Guildhall Road during 1925. During the year, the private hire and excursion work significantly expanded.

J. Jolton of Bradden introduced a service between Slapton and Northampton, Plough Hotel. The service ran via Greens Norton, Towcester, Blisworth and Milton. This was short lived and ceased in 1926.

The operations of Elizabeth Tomkins of Cotton End, Northampton were acquired by W.A. Nightingale in 1925, this adding a second stage-carriage service running from Northampton, St John's Street to Cosgrove. The villages of Wootton, Collingtree Turn, Courteenhall, Roade, Ashton Hartwell, Salcey Forest, Hanslope and Castlethorpe were all served. Tomkins commenced operation in 1922.

A successful excursion and tour business was established by George Richardson in 1925. Unlike others, these departed from the Plough Hotel rather than the Market Square.

1925 saw the extension of Northampton Corporation's route 2 to Weston Favell after opposition was met in 1924. The extended service commenced operation in November.

1926

York Bros. introduced a regular summer service between Northampton and Great Yarmouth in 1926. Overcrowding at the Black Boy Hotel, Dychurch Lane terminus, led to York Bros. apply to use Derngate as a terminus, this being granted on 8 May 1926.

The operations of Arthur Bird were another to be acquired by Allchin & Son, being done in February 1926. Bird introduced a route between Northampton and Olney in 1922.

The Northampton to Creaton service operated by John 'Jack' Smith had been extended to Guilsborough by March 1926. It was at this time the route became a daily one.

An application was received by the Watch Committee from William Edwin Hobley in the autumn of 1926. He wished to ply for hire from Regent Square, operating a service to Guilsborough. This was granted on 11 October, the service running via Chapel Brampton, Spratton, Creaton and Hollowell.

The same month saw Agnes Minney's service (Yardley Hastings-Northampton) diverted within Northampton itself. The route served All Saints' Church, the Drapery and Sheep Street, before terminating at the Cross Keys public house.

Benjamin Hasker was known in Northampton before the First World War for building carts and wagons. After the war, he went on to build bus bodies. In December 1926, he purchased a second-hand chassis and built a body on it. After applying for a licence, Hasker operated excursions from the Market Square for a season or two.

As mentioned above, Allchin acquired the business of Hardwick & Mann in February 1926. A second business was A.W. Bird of Northampton, based in Foundry Street. This added a service from St John's Street to Olney, via Weston Underwood, Stoke Goldington and Hackleton. Alongside this route were a number of excursions and tours from Northampton Market Square. The stage-carriage service was short-lived; it is believed that it was merged into a similar service operated by Wesley of Stoke Goldington.

The competition on the Northampton to Duston route proved too much for Wharmsley in 1926. This led to the Violet service being withdrawn.

The Wootton to Northampton service operated by George Tomlin had its terminus moved from the Knightley Arms to Bridge Street by the Watch Committee in 1927. The service continued to operate for a while, but no applications were made under the 1930 Road Traffic Act.

1926 was the final year of the Earls Barton to Northampton service operated by Alfred Jackson. Jackson had died in 1921, the service being continued by his wife.

Little is known about the operation of Charles Burbidge of Northampton. He was a taxi proprietor who operated a bus from 1920. He did operate a number of excursions over the years. This was the same for Frederick Tarry of Bugbrooke. Originally being a carrier, he operated a bus service between Bugbrooke, Kislingbury and Northampton between 1926 and 1930. The Northampton terminus was at the Woolpack Inn on Bridge Street.

Northampton Corporation first floated the idea of replacing trams on the Far Cotton service in October 1926, but it was deemed the wrong time to do so. The Corporation also wished to operate buses between Kingsthorpe and Abington on market days, but nothing came to fruition.

1927

Alfred Turner of Milton Malsor was granted a licence to operate his service between Gayton and Northampton in March 1927. He had been operating this service since 1924 but was refused a licence at the time. From this date, he terminated his service in both Guildhall Road and Cattle Market Road.

Amy Ayres and Wallace Garfield had been operating private hire work since 1925. In March 1927 they applied for a Hackney Carriage Licence to operate a service from Cattle Market Road to the nearby villages of Hardingstone and Piddington.

William Hobley's Northampton to Guilsborough service was revised in May 1927 to include Monday to Saturday workers' services. The service on Wednesdays and Saturdays was also increased to provide extra services to Northampton Market. The services operated under the Graham Bus Service name. Hobley did not last long, but the date he ceased operation is unknown. The timings passed to the Northampton Motor Omnibus Company Limited in 1928.

The Northampton Watch Committee received an application from John 'Jack' Welton of Maidford to stand a bus in George Row, Northampton. This was, however, not possible, and an alternative stand was allocated to Welton in St Johns Street. From 16 May, he commenced his bus service from Maidford, Farthingstone, Litchborough, Bugbrooke and Kislingbury to Northampton, operating on Wednesdays, Saturdays and Sundays. The service was soon extended to Preston Capes, with a further Saturday only extension to Woodford Halse and Eydon. The route operated along a similar one provided by Kingston Bros. of Blakesley.

The terminus of Charles Chinn's Northampton to Towcester service was changed in 1927 to Guildhall Road. In June, another licence was granted to allow Chinn to use St John's Street or Cattle Market Road as a stand.

Francis Belgrove of Cold Higham applied to the Watch Committee in May 1927 to operate a service between Cold Higham, Fosters Booth, Ascote, Eastcote, Rothersthorpe and Northampton, George Row. Variations of this service were introduced, running via Towcester. This operated alongside a market day service which served Banbury Lane, Rothersthorpe and Tiffield.

Arthur Basford of Greens Norton was granted a Hackney Carriage Licence by Northampton Borough Council in May, for use of a 14-seat bus.

In July 1927, Walter Lawrence of Wappenham applied to the Watch Committee to operate a service from Cattle Market Road to Milton, Blisworth, Towcester, Abthorpe and Wappenham. This was duly granted.

The Northampton terminus of York Brothers' Cogenhoe service was moved from Derngate to Becketts Well on Houghton Road in July 1927. Yorks soon established a garage next to the Black Boy Inn on Dychurch Lane. After this date they began operating excursions and tours from Market Square.

In this year, Allchin commenced a weekly service between Northampton and the Devon town of Torquay. The previous October Allchin had set up a small operation in Torquay itself. From Whitsun 1927 Allchin inaugurated a daily service between Northampton, Wood Hill and London, Oxford Street, running via Dunstable.

A second daily service between Northampton and London commenced operation in October 1927. At this time Nightingale & Sons operated the route, serving Towcester, Stony Stratford, Dunstable and St Albans. This service used Abington Street as a terminus. A year later, the route was operating under the Midland Motorway name.

In December 1927 an application to the Watch Committee was made by Albert Shaw of Harlestone to operate a service between St Andrews Road, Northampton, New Duston, Harlestone (Fox & Hounds), Upper Harlestone, Great Brington and Little Brington; the licence being granted the same month.

The Squirrels Bus Service moved their Northampton terminus from St Andrews Road to land located at the rear of the Black Boy Garage, Dychurch Lane. William Thomas Benson left the company at this time, the business passing to his son who named it Benson Bros. This was short-lived, ceasing in late 1927.

The end of 1927 also saw the private hire and excursion operation, along with the route between Northampton and Old operated by Henry Woolley & Son of Northampton, cease.

Walter Lawrence of Wappenham established a service between the village and Northampton, serving Towcester on its way. The service operated in competition with a similar service established by Frederick George Archer in 1914.

Law & Sons of Brafield extended their Northampton to Grendon service eastwards to the villages of Easton Maudit and Bozeat in 1927. The original terminus was located at Derngate, moving to Becketts Well/Bedford Road in 1928.

John George Ambrose Smith was the son of John 'Jack' Smith. In 1927, John Smith inaugurated a service from Cottesbrooke to the Cross Keys Hotel located in Sheep Street, Northampton. Running on a Wednesday, Friday and Saturday, the route followed a similar path to his father's route, through Creaton, Spratton, Chapel Brampton and Kingsthorpe.

Percival Clement Williams was the proprietor of the Angel Hotel, Bridge Street, Northampton. He applied for a Hackney Carriage Licence in 1927 to operate a horse-bus service for patrons of the hotel, linking with Northampton's Castle Station. The licence expired in March 1928 and was not renewed.

On an unknown date between 1925 and 1927, United Counties introduced a second service between Wellingborough and Northampton. Numbered 2A the route operated via Great Doddington, Earls Barton, Sywell, Overstone and Moulton.

1928

The Northampton Watch Committee granted a licence to Brown and Wilkinson of Grendon in December 1927 to operate a service between Grendon and Northampton. This was short-lived and was not renewed after the licence expired in March 1928.

The Northampton Borough Council Watch Committee revised the stands used by buses in Northampton during January 1928. Agnes Minney's Yardley Hastings to Northampton service was altered to terminate at Becketts Well in Houghton Road. The route was also extended at this time to the Buckinghamshire village of Lavendon, soon being extended further into Bedfordshire, to the village of Harrold.

On 26 May 1928, the operations of the Northampton Motor Omnibus Co. Ltd passed to United Counties. Prior to this, the Northampton to Harrold service passed to the National Omnibus Company who took the opportunity to extend it to Bedford. The sale was complete on 20 July, with six services being taken over by United Counties. These were:

Route 1 (Northampton (St Andrews Road)-Kislingbury Turn-Upper Heyford-Flore-Weedon-Dodford-Daventry, Market Square)
3 (Northampton (St Andrews Road)-Dallington-New Duston-Harlestone-Althorp-East Haddon-Long Buckby/West Haddon)
4 (Northampton (Guildhall Road)-Wootton-Courteenhall-Roade-Stoke Bruerne-Grafton Regis-Yardley Gobion-Potterspury-Old Stratford-Stony Stratford (Cock Hotel)
5 (Northampton (Regent Square)-Boughton-Pitsford-Brixworth-Lamport-Maidwell-Kelmarsh-Great Oxenden-Market Harborough)
6 (Northampton (Regent Square)-Chapel Brampton-Spratton-Creaton-Guilsborough-Thornby-Welford)
8 (Northampton (St Andrews Road)-Kislingbury Turn-Upper Heyford-Flore-Weedon-Upper Weedon-Everdon-Newnham-Badby).

These routes were renumbered 11, 13, 14, 12, 16 and 15.

Frederick Whitlock of Towcester abandoned his bus operations in June. It is believed that Walter Lawrence of Wappenham took over this operation. This included a route between Towcester and Northampton. This was soon extended to Lois Weedon and Weston-by-Weedon, with some journeys being diverted via Slapton, Bradden and Greens Norton.

John Smith extended his Northampton to Guilsborough service in June 1928 to serve Thornby and Naseby. From an unknown date, a Tuesday shoppers' service was introduced to Market Harborough.

Arthur Roberts of Gayton applied to the Watch Committee in July 1928 to stand a bus in St Johns Street. This allowed Roberts to inaugurate a service between Gayton, Blisworth, Milton and Northampton.

The Northampton to Moreton Pinkney service operated by Coombs & Sons passed to Harry Webster of Eastcote in March. Coombs continued running private hire work until 1929, when he sold out to W.A. Nightingale. The route inherited by Webster ran via Cold Higham, Fosters Booth, Pattishall, Astcote, Eastcote and Rothersthorpe.

Arthur Puttnam of Farthingstone commenced operation of a service between Farthingstone and the Plough Hotel, Northampton in 1928. This service operated on Wednesdays, Saturdays and Sundays. It served Church Stowe, Nether Heyford and the A45.

Joseph Whitlock left Northamptonshire during the first part of 1928. This led to the withdrawal of his Greens Norton to Northampton service.

The Northampton to Little Brington service of Albert Shaw referred to under the 1927 heading failed to generate sufficient revenue. As a result, the service ceased at the end of 1928. Another service to cease operation was the one between Gayton, Milton and Northampton operated by Alfred Turner.

A service was established between Brixworth, Pitsford, Boughton and Northampton in early 1928 by Joseph White of Brixworth.

April 1928 saw changes to Northampton Corporation Tramways route 2. A second, alternative, version, was added and was routed via Park Avenue North, Lindsay Avenue and Norman Road. The normal Wellingborough Road to Weston Favell route continued unaltered. A month later, route 1 (St James Road to Abington) was extended to terminate at the Five Bells Public House in Kingsthorpe. The Tramways Committee deemed the tram tracks on Wellingborough Road to be beyond economic repair in 1928. The choice at hand to the Committee at this time was to either renew the infrastructure or buy a fleet of double-deck buses. The Committee also had to take into consideration the growing housing areas under construction less than a mile away from the tram terminus in the Abington area of the town. J.F. Cameron, the General Manager of Northampton Corporation Tramways at this time, proposed an experiment in which tri-axle double-deck buses would compete with the trams along the Wellingborough Road route in order to compare them.

1929

On an unknown date between 1926 and 1929, Weedon-based Clarke Bros. extended their Northampton to Lower Weedon service to Daventry.

A new workers' service between Pattishall, Towcester and Northampton, Plough Hotel was introduced on Mondays to Saturdays by Bernard Reeve in April 1929.

The impending regulation of bus services resulted in Charlie Billington, owner of the Shakespeare Omnibus Company, selling his business in 1929. He reached an agreement with United Counties on 24 September for them to purchase his services but not his vehicles. He continued to use a couple of his vehicles on private hire work until 1930. His route between the Shakespeare Inn, Marefair and Duston (St Crispin's Hospital or Rifle Butt) were added to United Counties existing service 21, which operated a similar route.

York Bros. of Cogenhoe extended their Northampton to Cogenhoe service eastwards to Grendon and Wollaston in this year. A similar service was being provided at this time by J. Law of Brafield.

The Towcester to Northampton service provided by Charlie Chinn of Towcester was proving to be unreliable by 1929. This led passengers to approach Arthur Basford about providing an alternative service, which he did. Soon after this started, Chinn ceased operating.

Rance of Greens Norton commenced operation of a service between his home village and Northampton, via Towcester, Blisworth and the A43. Starting in 1929, it had ceased by 1930; little is known about this operation.

Allchin extended his Northampton to London service northwards in 1929, serving Leicester, Loughborough and Nottingham. This route was complemented by a feeder service operating between Northampton, Wellingborough and Kettering. The Northampton to Bournemouth service operated by Allchin began to run twice weekly during the winter.

The Midland Red Omnibus Company of Birmingham renumbered its service between Birmingham Bull Ring and Northampton on 2 February to the X96. The route also served Coventry, Binley, Wolston, Rugby and West Haddon. The route had been introduced in December 1928, numbered the 196. From 31 May a slight route deviation took place between Coventry and Wolston when it was rerouted to serve Willenhall and Ryton.

After the successful trial of the two Guy FCX double-deck buses on Northampton Corporation Tramways' Wellingborough Road route, the Corporation took the decision to replace the trams on this route. This introduced a new route 1, operating along the Wellingborough Road.

1930–1939

1930

Ernest Jeffrey Gibson applied to the Watch Committee in March 1930 to operate a service between Grendon and Northampton, standing the bus in Campbell Square. The licence was granted, but the service was short-lived, with Gibson making no application to the Traffic Commissioner for a Road Service Licence. York Bros. had commenced a service over the same route in 1929.

From 7 June, Wilfred Gibson of Walgrave commenced a weekend coach service between Northampton and Blackpool. The service also called at Leicester, Derby, Ashbourne, Leek, Macclesfield, Warrington, Wigan and Preston. The route operated Fridays, Sundays and Mondays. Again, no application was made for a Road Service Licence in 1931.

Allchin's Luxury Coaches expanded their network of express services in 1930. Firstly, the Nottingham-Leicester-Northampton-London service changed its terminus from Oxford Street to Charing Cross/Embankment. The Kettering feeder service was extended to also serve Thrapston, Oundle and Peterborough. Two additional feeder services were introduced to connect with the London service at Northampton. The first ran from Northampton to Rugby, Coventry, Nuneaton and Hinckley; the second connecting Daventry, Leamington Spa, Warwick, Birmingham and Wolverhampton.

Allchin also operated a number of coastal services in 1930. The first ran between Northampton and Bournemouth/Portsmouth via Oxford, Abingdon, Newbury, Winchester and Southampton; the second between Northampton, London, Brighton, Eastbourne and Hastings. A third, weekend only, service ran between Northampton, London, Margate and Ramsgate. Perhaps the longest of the services ran between Northampton, Warwick, Stratford-upon-Avon, Tewkesbury, Gloucester, Bristol, Taunton, Exeter, Teignmouth, Torquay, Paignton and Plymouth. The final service linked Northampton with Great Yarmouth and Lowestoft, running via Bedford, Cambridge and Norwich.

29 December 1930 saw United Counties take several routes from Clarke Bros. of Weedon. The latter company was operating a route between Daventry and Northampton; Upper Weedon and Northampton and a third between Weedon and Northampton. These were absorbed into United Counties' existing services. Clarke Bros. continued to operate their Daventry to Rugby service at this time.

The Wappenham to Northampton service operated by Frederick George Archer ceased operating by the end of 1930.

Amy Ayres' service between Piddington, Hardingstone and Northampton had significantly grown by 1930, with the terminus moving from Cattle Market Road to the Plough Hotel.

During the year, the terminus of Kingston Bros.' Woodend to Northampton service moved to Cattle Market Road. It was also at this time that the route was diverted to serve Canons Ashby and Moreton Pinkney.

Sarah Knight's Sally Omnibus Service was the dominant operator on the Northampton to Yardley Hastings service by 1930. Knight invested in new rolling stock, forcing Agnes Minney to do the same, this putting financial strain on Minney. In 1930, Agnes Minney sold her business to Knight, including her Northampton to Harrold service.

The Bozeat to Northampton service operated by Andrew Law & Sons had its Northampton terminus moved to Cheyne Walk, this being the fourth terminus in the town used by Law.

Midland Red's service X96 (Birmingham Bull Ring-Northampton) was extended in April 1930 to Shrewsbury. The route also served Dudley, Wolverhampton and Wellington on its way. It continued to operate like this with little change until the late 1960s.

On 16 July, Northampton Corporation made the decision to replace the trams on the Kettering Road service with buses. It was proposed for the new bus route to operate from All Saints' Church in the town centre, along Kettering Road to its junction with Park Avenue North. They also proposed to extend route 1 into the new Abington housing estate. Instead of these, an experimental circular service was introduced, running from All Saints' Church along Wellingborough Road and Park Avenue North, terminating at Lindsay Avenue. It then returned along Kettering Road on its way back to the town centre. This new service commenced operation on 1 September, being withdrawn in December. September saw route 2 (Wood Hill-Weston Favell) routed via Briton Road and Norman Road to reach the latter terminus. In December, the Town Centre-Wellingborough Road-Lindsay Avenue section of the service retained route number 1, whilst the Kettering Road service was numbered 2, terminating at the Golf House.

1931

As mentioned in the introduction, 1931 saw the introduction of the 1930 Road Traffic Act which required operators to apply to the Traffic Commissioner for a Road Service Licence to continue operating their services.

The impending introduction of this Act resulted in no less than six independent operators who were operating into Northampton selling their business to United Counties. The first takeover took place on 19 March when Wallace and Amy Ayres of Hardingstone sold up to United Counties. Their service between Northampton, Hardingstone and Wootton was allocated route number 24 by the new owner.

On 25 March, the business of John 'Jack' Smith (Blue Fly Service) of Creaton was acquired. Smith had operated a service between Creaton, Spratton, Chapel Brampton and Northampton since 1924. The acquisition allowed United Counties to increase its timings on route 16 and introduce a Tuesday only service (16A) between Northampton, Guilsborough, Sibbertoft and Market Harborough.

Thomas Miller made his applications to the Traffic Commissioner. However, before these were granted, he was approached by United Counties with regard to taking over his operations. They did so from 1 September, by which time his original service was extended to Naseby. Two of Miller's four services were acquired, Welford to Northampton and Welford to Market Harborough.

In September, Maurice Spruels of Scaldwell was operating services between Old and Northampton, and between Old and Kettering. Both applications were withdrawn before being granted. Spruels was acquired by United Counties on 17 October, the deal including the Sunday only service between Old, Scaldwell, Brixworth and Northampton.

G.W. Frisby was another operator to be subsumed by United Counties during 1931. On 16 November, the Kettering to Northampton service was transferred. On this date, United Counties also took over the operation of Albert Owen Clarke, who was operating a service between Moulton and Campbell Square, Northampton. Clarke had made an application to the Traffic Commissioner prior to the takeover, this being withdrawn.

In April, Arthur Basford, the Kingston Bros., William Nutt, Allchin's Luxury Coaches, Samuel Kirton and Abram all applied to the Traffic Commissioner for Road Service Licences. Arthur Basford applied to continue operating his services between Paulerspury, Shutlanger, Blisworth and Northampton; and Greens Norton, Towcester, Blisworth and Northampton. Kingston Bros. was granted permission to operate their Woodend to Northampton service in June 1931. Harpole-based William Nutt applied for four licences, these all being granted. These were to continue operating services between Great Brington-Northampton; Little Brington-Northampton and Harpole-Northampton. The fourth was for a daily service between Norton, Whilton Locks, Little Brington, Nobottle, Old Duston and Northampton. By 1931, Samuel Kirton had extended his service to Fosters Booth. The application for this service was eventually granted in September.

Allchin applied for a number of licences, with only around half of those applied for being granted. Those that were refused were on the basis that other provisions were already in place. The licences that were granted were for services between Derby and Northampton; Nottingham and Warwick; Nottingham and Hastings; Nottingham and Bournemouth; Nottingham and Lowestoft; Nottingham and London; Northampton and Birmingham; Northampton and Torquay; Northampton and Peterborough and Northampton and Skegness, along with excursions and tours from Northampton.

W.A. Nightingale made his application in May. In July, a licence for the Northampton to Cosgrove service was granted; whilst the licence for the Northampton, Towcester, London service was granted in September. It took until November before Nightingale gained a licence for his Northampton-Towcester-Silverstone service.

Abram was not keen on the idea of the introduction of the Road Traffic Act, and in December 1930 approached United Counties with the view of the latter concern taking over his services. However, nothing came of this, and Abram was forced to apply for licences from 1 April. At this time, he was operating three stage carriage services, one of these being a Saturday only service between Earls Barton and Northampton between September and April. He went on to apply for a licence between Market Square and Towcester Races on Easter Monday and Tuesday. The first was granted, the second being refused.

F.E. Beeden made his application during July to continue operation of the bus services mentioned under the 1920s heading. At the same time, he applied to operate excursions and tours from Northampton Market Square. These licences were all granted in November.

In August, applications were received from George Blundell of Spratton, John George Ambrose Smith, Arthur Walker and George Richardson of Hartwell. Blundell applied for two licences, the first for his Northampton to Spratton service.

The second was for an excursions and tours licence. The first was granted, whilst the latter application was withdrawn. John George Ambrose Smith applied to continue operating his Cottesbrooke to Northampton service, the licence being granted in November. Arthur Walker also had his licences granted in November, allowing him to continue operating excursions and tours from Northampton to Hunstanton and Great Yarmouth, along with tours to Stratford-on-Avon. By 1932, Walker ceased operation. George Richardson was granted licences to continue operating routes between Northampton and Hartwell/Hanslope and Northampton and Collingtree, on Wednesdays, Saturdays and Sundays.

Bernard Reeve applied in September to continue to operate his Grimscote to Northampton service, running via Pattishall, Astcote, Eastcote and Rothersthorpe, this being granted in November. He also applied for a licence for a new service between Pattishall, Towcester, Blisworth and Northampton, this covering his workers' service. This was withdrawn in January 1932. Towards the end of 1931, Reeve was declared bankrupt, his debt being cleared by his uncle, W.A. Nightingale. The latter proprietor applied to the Traffic Commissioner to take over Reeves' services, but the unreliability and the fact that his services were provided by other operators meant that the application was refused.

The Leathersich Brothers applied for their Road Service Licence in the autumn. This was granted, the route operating between Old, Walgrave, Harrington, Holcot, Moulton and Northampton, the terminus being at the Stag's Head on Abington Street, with permission being granted to use Campbell Square. At this time, the name Red Bus Service was being used.

The autumn also saw Samuel Walters of Helmdon apply for a licence to continue operating a service between Greatworth and Northampton, this being granted. At the time it was granted, the Northampton terminus was the Bull & Butcher.

Several licences were applied for by Walter Lawrence in October and November. The first was for the Wednesday, Saturday and Sunday only service between Weston-by-Weedon and Northampton. A restriction was placed on this service that no local passengers could be carried between Towcester and Northampton. The second was the Wednesday and Saturday service between Wappenham, Slapton, Bradden, Greens Norton, Duncote, Towcester, Blisworth, Milton and Northampton, Plough Hotel, with the same restrictions being imposed. Lawrence applied in November to operate a Thursday evening service between Wappenham and Market Square, this being granted in December. Unlike his other services, he was allowed to carry local passengers between Towcester and Northampton.

Sarah Knight had a licence granted for her Northampton-Yardley Hastings/Harrold service in November. At the time it was granted, the route terminated at Derngate and served Great and Little Houghton, Brafield, Denton, Yardley Hastings, Olney and Lavendon.

Andrew Law & Sons had their licence for the Bozeat to Northampton service granted by the Traffic Commissioner during November. This was also the case for Jack Welton of Maidford, who was granted permission to continue operating into Northampton.

York Bros. gained a licence in December to continue operating their seasonal service between Northampton and Great Yarmouth. By this time, the route was operating Fridays, Saturdays, Sundays and Mondays. It was after this date that York Bros. traded as the Easy Motor Coach Co.

At the same time, Joseph White of Brixworth applied to operate two stage-carriage services. The first operated between Kingsthorpe Cemetery and Northampton, providing workers' journeys for the Northampton shoe factories. The second ran between Northampton, Brixworth, Lamport, Maidwell and Haselbech. They had both been granted by January 1932.

William Jackson was granted a licence on 17 December to operate between Northampton, Boughton, Pitsford and Brixworth.

Wilfred Gibson of Walgrave was granted a licence to operate his service between Old and Northampton, along with his lunchtime service for the Sears Shoe factory in Northampton. Francis Belgrove placed an application for three licences during 1931 to operate his services between Cold Higham and Northampton. The first served Fosters Booth, Astcote, Towcester, Blisworth and Milton, terminating at Bridge Street Car Park; the second served Fosters Booth, Pattishall, Astcote, Caldcote, Tiffield, Blisworth and Milton before terminating in Northampton. The third ran along a similar route, serving Fosters Booth, Pattishall, Astcote, Eastcote and Rothersthorpe.

Sydney Charles Kingston applied to operate a number of services, one of which operated into Northampton. The route concerned ran between the town and Syresham. Arthur Roberts of Gayton also applied to continue operating his Gayton to Northampton service. This was also the case for Alfred Roland Surridge who applied to operate his Northampton-Upton-Harpole service, these all being granted.

Alfred Looker ceased operation of his West Hadden to Northampton service by the time the Road Traffic Act came into effect.

To reflect the operation of buses by Northampton Corporation Transport Tramways, the company changed their name to Northampton Corporation Transport in 1931.

1932

George Richardson became the first of many Northamptonshire independent operators to be acquired by United Counties during 1932 after approaching the company in January. At this time, Richardson's services were incorporated into United Counties' network.

Joseph White applied to operate two midday shoe workers services in January 1932, both of which were granted. Both operated to Kingsthorpe, the first from the Dover factory in St James, the second from the Lotus factory in Victoria Street. White sold his business to United Counties in February, with the stage services and workers' services continuing.

In February, the Northampton to Hanslope service operated by W.A. Nightingale was co-ordinated with a similar service operated by G.E. Richardson of Hartwell. The latter operator's route continued past Hanslope to serve Castlethorpe and Wolverton. At this time, Richardson was in financial difficulties and had entered negotiations with United Counties who had come to an agreement. This made the Nightingale service attractive to United Counties, and in February 1932 they made an application to acquire the Northampton to Towcester route of Richardson. On 21 March, the licence was granted, and the route was numbered 26, linking Northampton, Roade and Wolverton.

Alfred Surridge was granted a short-term licence in March 1932 to operate a lunchtime workers' service between the Marlow & Sons factory in St George Street to Junction Road. A full licence for the route was granted in August.

Abram approached United Counties for a second time in March 1932 with a view to selling his business and assets. A deal was signed between the two concerns on 23 March, with United Counties taking over the business in April 1932. The deal included a route between Irthlingborough and Northampton, and an excursions and tours licence. The services were taken on from 4 May, the sale being officially completed on 30 May.

Thomas George Lamb of Byfield applied to the Traffic Commissioner a lot later than most operators in the Northampton area, doing so in March 1932. One of his services operated into the area of study in this book, running between Byfield and Northampton. It serviced the villages of Woodford Halse, Preston Capes, Maidford, Litchborough, Bugbrooke and Kislingbury. The licence was granted in June, with a condition being applied to the Northampton route, that passengers were not allowed to be picked up or set down between Bugbrooke and Northampton. One journey in each direction was provided on Wednesdays and Saturdays.

Another lunchtime workers' service commenced operation in May 1932. William Nutt of Harpole started a few services for both C&E Lewis and Padmore & Barnes. The route for the former factory ran between St James and Campbell Square; whilst the latter ran between Countess Road and Weston Favell. A short-term licence was granted, but a long-term licence was refused after objections were made by Northampton Corporation.

Although Jack Welton of Maidford and Kingston Bros. of Woodend had been competing on a service between Maidford and Northampton since 1927, the pair teamed up in June 1932 to form a new company, KW Services. From this date, the new Company operated two services into the County Town. The first operated from Woodend to Northampton via Blakesley, Maidford, Adstone, Canons Ashby, Moreton Pinkney, Culworth and Thorpe Mandeville. The second ran between Eydon, Woodford Halse, Preston Capes, Maidford, Farthingstone, Litchborough, Bugbrooke, Kislingbury and Northampton. Changes to the Bugbrooke to Northampton section saw co-operative working on the route with United Counties.

Between June and November, United Counties acquired five local businesses. The first was of Brixworth-based William Jackson on 20 June. The Northampton to Brixworth service was incorporated into United Counties' existing service.

Some weeks later, on 14 July, Herbert Phillips of Long Buckby also sold his service between his home village and Northampton to United Counties. Again, the route was incorporated into United Counties' existing service between the two locations. From 27 August, United Counties took over the service of George Blundell between Northampton and Spratton after he approached the former operator earlier in the month.

An agreement was reached in September between John Smith and United Counties for the latter to take over operation of the Cottesbrooke to Northampton service, this taking place on 1 October. From this date, United Counties diverted route 16 to serve Cottesbrooke on Wednesdays and Saturdays.

The operations of Wilfred Gibson and Leathersich Bros. came to the attention of United Counties during 1932. An agreement was reached between Gibson and United Counties on 25 November for the purchase of the Old to Northampton service. A licence for this service was granted from 1 January 1933. Gibson retained his vehicles, continuing to operate private hire work until 1933.

F&E Beeden amalgamated the two licences held for the Towcester and Wappenham services during the second part of 1932. By this time, Beeden was also operating services out to the Towcester Races.

During the 1920s and early 1930s, Charles Wilford of Northampton operated a number of excursions from Northampton Market Square. A couple of lunchtime services were also operated by Wilford at this time serving the shoe factories. In 1932, an application was made to continue these services. They ran between Manfield Road and Campbell Square, the other between Stimpson Avenue and Far Cotton. The operation was sold to Knights of Denton in 1935.

Samuel Kirton applied for a licence to operate his lunchtime services between the Cowper Factory on Shakespeare Road and Park Road, St James. These were duly granted.

Long Buckby-based Herbert Phillips introduced a second service from his home village to Northampton in 1932. This Sunday only service passed through the villages of Ravensthorpe, East Haddon, Holdenby, Church Brampton and Kingsthorpe, terminating in Northampton at the Bull Hotel.

Mayfair Transport Company Ltd of Kilburn, London had operated an express service between London, St Albans, Dunstable, Fenny Stratford, Stony Stratford, Towcester, Northampton, Market Harborough and Leicester. One journey each way was operated. In April 1931, Mayfair entered receivership and United Counties made an application to take over the service. However, objections were met from the LM&S Railway, Allchin and Leicester Corporation, the licence subsequently being refused. In October, Allchin Luxury Coaches also applied for a licence for a similar service, this again being refused because of objections from the LM&S Railway, as well as Nightingales and Midland Red, again leading to the withdrawal of the application.

A similar saga presented itself in March and April 1932 when United Counties, with the agreement of Nightingale & Sons, applied to the Traffic Commissioner to take over Nightingale's Northampton, Towcester, Dunstable, London service. The LM&S Railway, Allchin's, F&E Beeden and S.C. Kingston of Silverstone all voiced objections. United Counties eventually withdrew the application in November 1932. Allchin & Sons applied for a licence in May, to operate the Northampton to Hockliffe portion of Nightingale's route. This was granted in October 1933, and a daily service commenced.

United Counties expanded further during 1932 with ten independent operators being acquired, with an agreement reached with Joseph Herbert White of Brixworth in March. At the time of acquisition, White was operating a service between Brixworth and Northampton; workers' services within the town as well as tours and excursions from Brixworth. From 25 March, the Brixworth service was incorporated into United Counties' existing service.

The joint service of G.E. Richardson and W.A. Nightingale, running between Northampton, Wootton, Roade, Hanslope and Wolverton, was acquired in April. United Counties came to an agreement with W.A. Nightingale on the operation of the route.

April also saw the acquisition of the business of Joseph Charles Abram of Earls Barton. From 4 April, Abram's route between Northampton, Earls Barton and Wellingborough was taken over.

In 1932, William Jackson, also of Brixworth, made the decision to sell to United Counties. The deal was complete on 1 July, after which time his Brixworth to Northampton, Regent Square service was incorporated into United Counties' own service. On 31 July, Herbert Phillip of Long Buckby sold his business to United Counties. The acquisition of this business gave United Counties the opportunity to increase its timings on route 13, as well as introduce new route 28 between Northampton, Chapel Brampton, Church Brampton, Holdenby, East Haddon, Ravensthorpe, Long Buckby, Norton and Daventry. It was at this time an outstation was established in Long Buckby.

The following month, George Blundell of Spratton sold out to United Counties. This added a service between Spratton and Northampton to United Counties' portfolio in August.

John George Ambrose Smith's Blue Fly Service was the final operator to be acquired by United Counties during 1932. Smith's service between Cottesbrooke and the Cross Keys Hotel, Northampton was incorporated into United Counties' service 16 from 1 October.

In the early part of 1932, United Counties withdrew route 2A from Moulton, using the main road instead to enter Northampton.

Alterations were made to Northampton Corporation's services from 1 April. Alternate journeys on the Wellingborough Road service (route 1) were extended from Abington Park to either Lindsay Avenue or Weston Favell. The new route 2, which operated along Kettering Road, saw alternate journeys terminate at either St Matthew's Church or the Golf House. It was at this time that the terminus of the original route 2 (Wood Hill-Abington Park-Briton Road) was curtailed back to Abington Park, this route serving Billing Road. By 1932, Northampton Corporation were also providing a number of lunchtime services around the town for various factories.

1933

The Byfield to Northampton service operated by T.G. Lamb of Byfield was incorporated into the Eydon to Northampton service operated by KW Services. Lamb continued operating his Eydon to Banbury service for another year before it passed to Midland Red. KW Services applied for two Road Service Licences in May 1933 for two stage carriage services. The first was a Wednesday only service between Little Preston, Preston Capes, Adstone, Maidford, Farthingstone, Litchborough, Bugbrooke and Northampton. The second was a Wednesday and Saturday only service between Woodford and Northampton, serving Blakesley, Foxley, Fosters Booth and Rothersthorpe. These were granted, with restrictions on loading passengers between Bugbrooke and Northampton.

An agreement was reached between York Bros. and J&A Law of Brafield with the view to the former acquiring the latter operator's business. After applying to the Traffic Commissioner, objections were met from Sarah Knight with regards to the Brafield to Northampton service. An agreement was reached between York Bros. and Knight, with Yorks having restrictions placed on them about setting down and picking up passengers between Brafield and Northampton. Knight paid a sum to both Law and York Bros., who in return would not take local passengers. The licence was eventually granted in June 1933, at which time Andrew Law & Sons ceased operation. Soon after acquisition, the route was amended by Yorks to operate between Northampton and Wollaston via the Houghtons, Brafield, Cogenhoe, Whiston, Castle Ashby, Grendon, Easton Maudit and Bozeat. The other service ran between Northampton, Little Billing and Cogenhoe before following this line of route to Wollaston.

William Nutt applied to operate a workers' service between Countess Road and Kingsley Road (Hatton's Shoe Co. Ltd) in September, this being granted.

On 1 October 1933, the Northampton to London express service operated by Nightingales passed to Allchin & Son of Northampton. At the same time, United Counties purchased the Northampton, Towcester, Silverstone route from Nightingale.

Francis Belgrove extended his Northampton to Cold Higham service to the village of Grimscote during 1933.

Seven independent operators were acquired by United Counties during 1933. In 1932, the businesses of both Leathersich Bros. and Wilfred Gibson, both based in Walgrave, became of interest to United Counties. Negotiations began in December 1932 with the Leathersich Bros., these concluding in January 1933. Trading as the Red Bus Service, they operated a service between Old and Northampton, Race Horse Inn, Abington Square. The service called at Walgrave, Hannington, Holcot and Moulton between the two locations. Gibson also operated a service between Old and Northampton, as well as workers' services within Northampton. The Old-Walgrave-Northampton service of both operators were given route number 29 with United Counties.

Allchin Luxury Coaches of Northampton sold their business to United Counties from 1 December. This included thirty-one vehicles. Allchin continued operating his Torquay-based business. By the time Allchin was taken over, they had developed a good network of long-distance express services based on Northampton. United Counties took over the following routes:

- Nottingham–Loughborough–Leicester–Northampton–Newport Pagnell–Dunstable-London
- Nottingham–Loughborough–Leicester–Northampton–London–Brighton–Eastbourne–Hastings
- Nottingham–Loughborough–Leicester–Northampton–Oxford–Southampton–Bournemouth
- Nottingham–Loughborough–Leicester–Northampton–Cambridge–Norwich–Great Yarmouth–Lowestoft
- Birmingham–Coventry–Rugby–Northampton
- Derby–Loughborough–Leicester–Northampton
- Northampton–Wellingborough–Kettering–Peterborough
- Northampton–Stamford–Spalding–Skegness
- Northampton–Daventry–Warwick–Tewkesbury–Gloucester–Bristol–Taunton–Exeter–Dawlish–Teignmouth–Newton Abbot–Torquay

Northampton Corporation replaced the tram tracks outside of All Saints' Church on the Far Cotton Line in August 1933. For the duration of these works, trams were replaced by buses, three being hired from Aldershot & District. These moved on to the Kingsthorpe route after the Far Cotton work had been completed. The track on the Kingsthorpe route was also in need of repair, but Northampton Borough Council decided not to replace it. Instead, after weighing up a number of options including a trolleybus route, buses were chosen to replace trams on the route. They arrived in September 1933, the new route commencing on the 27th. It was at this time that the route was extended to the Five Bells Public House.

1934

The terminus of Samuel Kirton's service between Fosters Booth and Northampton moved to St John's Street on Mondays, Tuesdays, Thursdays and Fridays, remaining at the Bull and Butcher on the other days. It later moved permanently to The Mayorhold, before moving to the Plough Hotel, Bridge Street in 1938.

Sarah Knight expanded her business during 1934, by successfully gaining licences for excursions from Northampton.

George Leonard Edward's Northampton to Paulerspury service was extended in 1934 to serve Towcester on Saturday evenings. He also applied to operate a similar service on Friday evenings, this being granted but on the condition that passengers were carried end to end only, following objection from the railways.

United Counties was again looking to expand during 1934. The first was the business of William Nutt of Harpole (Bluebell Motor Services). The deal was completed on 24 January, at which time a new service was introduced numbered 57, running between Northampton and Harpole. At the same time, a Wednesday, Saturday and Sunday service between Northampton and Whilton Locks was introduced, numbered 58. A route between Northampton and Daventry had been operating for many years, but it had not been diverted into Harpole.

April 1932 had seen United Counties acquire the Northampton to Wolverton service of W.A. Nightingale. They also wanted to operate the Northampton to London service, but the application was refused by the Traffic Commissioner. Nightingale also operated other stage-carriage services, these becoming of interest to United Counties. After negotiations, United Counties acquired Nightingale's business on 5 February 1934. Two new routes were introduced at this time to incorporate them. The 53 ran between Northampton, Milton, Blisworth, Towcester, Silverstone and Syresham. The 54 operated between Towcester, Ascote, Pattishall, Fosters Booth and Cold Higham.

Sidney Kingston jointly operated the Northampton to Syresham service with Nightingale. United Counties acquired Kingston's business on the same day as Nightingale's. Kingston's garage was taken on by United Counties, establishing an outstation in Silverstone.

United Counties acquired three operators in the Buckingham area in June, with a couple of services crossing the border into Northamptonshire. Joseph Dunkley (Old Joe) operated a route between Buckingham and Northampton operating on Wednesdays, calling at Towcester on its way through. Lewis Tibbets of Akeley also operated a bus service between Buckingham, Towcester and Northampton. Unlike Dunkley, Tibbets operated on both Wednesdays and Saturdays. The third operator was A.J. and A.G. Varney of Buckingham. Varney again operated a route between Buckingham, Towcester and Northampton. These services were incorporated into United Counties' existing service 49, this originally running between Aylesbury and Buckingham. It was extended northwards from Buckingham to Whittlebury, Towcester, Blisworth and Northampton.

1934 was the last year of operation of the tram network in Northampton. In July, Northampton Corporation made the decision to replace trams on both the St James and Far Cotton services with buses. The last tram operated on 15 December. The withdrawal of the trams saw the Far Cotton to Kingsthorpe and St James to Kettering Road services operate as through services. Extensions were made to the routes to Rothersthorpe Road and Abbots Way.

1935

Sarah Knight purchased the operations of C. Wilford & Sons in April, this increasing the number of excursions operated from the Northampton area. Two lunchtime workers' services were also acquired by Knight, the first operating between Manfield Road and Campbell Square; the second between Stimpson Avenue and Far Cotton.

By 1935, a company called Empire's Best, based in Wood Green, London, were operating two express services. One of these operated between Clacton-on-Sea and Birmingham, passing through Haverhill, Cambridge, Bedford, Northampton, Leicester and Coventry. The popularity of the other service (London–Clacton) led to difficulties operating the Birmingham service. In late 1935, this route passed to Premier Travel of Cambridge, gaining route number 5.

Unlike previous years, United Counties only took over two independent operators during 1935. The first was the business of W.F. Pack of Brigstock. Although Pack's operations were centred on the Kettering area, one route is of interest for this book. He operated a service between Kettering and Deene via Geddington, Stanion, Weldon and Deenethorpe. The existing services 6 and 8 (Northampton–Stamford) were diverted on Friday to accommodate the service operating to Deene. The sale was complete on 1 February.

The second operator was Alfred Surridge of Harpole. At the time of takeover, Surridge was operating a service between Northampton and Harpole, alongside some shoe factory workers' services. These were taken on by United Counties.

Negotiations had been ongoing for several months between United Counties and Northampton Corporation Transport about the co-ordination of services in Northampton. A small measure was introduced from 14 January 1935. From this date, Northampton Corporation introduced a service to Manfield Hospital. It was agreed at this time that United Counties were able to charge the same fares as the Corporation but could not pick up or set down local passengers between Northampton and The Avenue, Spinney Hill. Although the hope was there, no further co-ordination between the two concerns was achieved until after the war.

February 1935 saw the express services inherited by United Counties in 1933 gain route numbers. These were as follows:

X1 Nottingham–Leicester–Northampton–London
X2 Nottingham–Leicester–Northampton–Brighton–Eastbourne–Hastings
X3 Nottingham–Leicester–Northampton–Great Yarmouth–Lowestoft
X4 Nottingham–Leicester–Northampton–Bournemouth
X5 Birmingham–Northampton
X7 Peterborough–Northampton
X9 Northants area–Whipsnade Zoo
X10 Northants area–Hunstanton
X11 Northants area–Mablethorpe
X12 Northants area–Great Yarmouth
X13 Northants area–Clacton

The Northampton to Torquay service passed to Associated Motorways in 1934, this also being the case for the Nottingham to Bournemouth service X4 in 1935.

Northampton Corporation re-organised its routes between St James, Abington and Billing Road in April 1935. These were numbered 8 and 9, joining at the Five Bells in Kingsthorpe. New route 7 was introduced to terminate at the junction of Towcester Road and Rothersthorpe Road. An experimental service was introduced in November 1935 after an approach by the Northampton Rate Payers Association. The route ran from St James Square to either Weedon Road and Abotts Way or Harlestone Road and Warren Road. These took up service numbers 6 and 12.

1936

KW Services applied for a licence for a service between Lower Heyford, Bugbrooke, Kislingbury and Northampton on a short-term basis in January 1936. It was granted to cover for a strike affecting United Counties. However, the latter operator and Northampton Corporation both objected, leading to the withdrawal of the application. At the same time, the restrictions imposed on KW Services on picking up and setting down passengers between Bugbrooke and Northampton were relaxed. The company became a Limited Company from 16 December.

Very little of interest happened concerning United Counties in the Northampton area during 1936. The X7 (Peterborough–Northampton) was withdrawn in July.

By March 1936, Northampton Corporation were operating twelve services. To summarise these, route 1 was operating between the town centre and Weston Favell. Route 2 operated to the Abington housing estate, the terminus being at Lindsay Avenue. Routes 3, 4 and 11 served Kettering Road, route 3 terminating at St Matthew's Church; route 4 terminated at the Golf House. Route 11 continued to terminate at Manfield Hospital. Routes 5, 8 and 9 served the Kingsthorpe area, all terminating at the Five Bells. The Far Cotton service had been numbered 7, whilst route 6 ran between the town centre and Abbots Way. The final service was the 12, operating to Warren Road.

Northampton Corporation wished to expand their network in 1936. They wanted to extend the Kingsthorpe route to the local cemetery; whilst they wanted to expand the Far Cotton service to Rothersthorpe Road, running via London Road and Queen Eleanor Road before passing through the nearby housing estate. Both proposals were refused by the Traffic Commissioner in September. A third proposal was made to extend the St James service out to Bant Lane. This too was refused after objection was met from United Counties.

1937

1937 was a quiet year for bus operations in Northampton. KW Services officially became a Limited Company in early 1937. New licences were applied for by the new operator, including one for excursions and tours; alongside several stage-carriage services linking Northampton, Plough Hotel with Woodend, Eydon and Little Preston.

Alfred Surridge made a brief return to the Northampton bus scene when, in May 1937, he helped out United Counties when staff went on strike. At this time, Surridge gained a short period licence to operate between New Duston and Northampton.

The terminus of Samuel Walter's Greatworth to Northampton service moved to the Bridge Street Car Park in the autumn of 1937.

Northampton Corporation introduced another new service on 12 September. The route ran between the town centre and Bush Hill, via Kettering Road, Ivy Road and Birchfield Road. Route number 10 was allocated to the service. This was the number used by private hire vehicles, these using number 20 thereafter.

1938

Arthur Basford applied for a licence in April 1938 to operate a new service between Greens Norton and Northampton, Bridge Street. It served the villages of Towcester,

Paulerspury, Heathencote, Shutlanger and Blisworth between the two locations. Certain journeys were extended to serve a number of shoe factories in Northampton.

The Paulerspury to Northampton service operated by George Leonard Edwards had its terminus moved to the yard of the Bull & Butcher in Bridge Street. A Friday-only parcel service was introduced over the route at the same time.

F&E Beeden was the last significant, independent operator based in Northampton by the late 1930s. Beeden entered negotiations with United Counties with an agreement being reached on 1 March 1938. The takeover was complete on 26 June, at which time Beeden's services were absorbed into United Counties' network. At the time of takeover, the following routes were operated by Beeden along with excursions and tours from Market Square:

- Northampton (Cattle Market Road)–Hardingstone–Hackleton–Stoke Goldington–Newport Pagnell
- Northampton (Cattle Market Road)–Hardingstone–Hackleton–Piddington–Horton Gates
- Northampton (Guildhall Road)–Milton–Blisworth–Towcester–Abthorpe–Wappenham
- Northampton (Guildhall Road)–Milton–Blisworth–Shutlanger–Heathencote–Paulerspury–Whittlebury

The Newport Pagnell and Horton Gates services were covered by an extension of route 24 from Wootton. The Wappenham service was absorbed into United Counties' route 53 (Northampton–Towcester–Syresham). The Northampton to Whittlebury route was given new service number 74. Routes 14, 26, 46 and 52 were also altered to incorporate some of Beeden's services.

The special dispensation given to Northampton Corporation by the Traffic Commissioner to operate single-decks with only a driver was withdrawn in May 1938. This affected routes 8 (Wood Hill–Kingsthorpe); route 9 (St James–Kingsthorpe) and route 10 (Town Centre–Bush Hill), as well as a number of midday workers' services. From this date, conductors were employed on single-decks. Service revisions were implemented from 29 May. Route 4 was extended from Northwood Road to Headlands, route 2 was re-routed to serve Wellingborough Road, Park Avenue North and Birchfield Road before reaching Bush Hill (Bushland Road). Route 10 was withdrawn at this time.

1939

In January 1939, Sarah Knight discontinued the workers' service between Stimpson Avenue and Far Cotton. The Manfield Road to Campbell Square service was taken over by United Counties. At this time, Sarah Knight and her husband Charles retired. The business passed to Charles Knight's brother Herbert Sidney Knight. A new company was formed, known as Knight's Coaches; more information can be found in the next chapter.

In 1939, the Easy Motor Coach Co. name was dropped by York Bros. The name York Bros. (Northampton) Ltd was used from this time. New licences had to be applied for. Two stage-carriage services were operated at this time: Northampton, Victoria Promenade–Wollaston, Northampton–Bozeat, and Northampton, Wood Hill to Great Yarmouth. Tours and excursions were also operated from Market Square.

1940–1949

1940–1945 The War Years

The years 1940 to 1945 are grouped together under one heading to help best describe the various operators' operations during the Second World War. To give full coverage of the war years, events concerning bus operations in Northampton that took place after war was declared on 3 September 1939 are also incorporated under this heading. During the Second World War, Northampton fared better than many other towns and cities close by, with few bombs falling on the town.

Knights Coaches, the former Sally Omnibus Service, continued to operate the excursions part of the business. The outbreak of war stopped this, but Knight played a big part in the local war effort. Knight helped to transport evacuees from Northampton Rail Station to locations around the county. He also operated contracts to transport military personnel from the Harrington base, as well as construction workers between Northampton and the Bedfordshire village of Podington, the location of an airfield that was under construction. A more unusual contract awarded to Knights was to transport a theatre company between Northampton and Coventry. The company also operated a contract to transport staff between George Row, Northampton and the Brooklands Aviation factory in Sywell; along with security staff between Northampton and the Yardley Chase Ammunition depot. In 1943, Sidney Knight took over the services of J.H. Mills of Brixworth who was operating a service between Brixworth and the Cross Keys public house in Sheep Street, Northampton.

Arthur Basford also gained a number of Defence Permits allowing him to carry workers who were assisting with the war effort in Northamptonshire, Oxfordshire and Buckinghamshire. Two of these concerned the Northampton area. The first was a Friday and Sunday evening airmen service between Silverstone Camp and Northampton Rail Station. A second similar service ran between Northampton Station and Whitchurch Camp, near to Aylesbury.

Norman Heeps, son of Albert Norman Heeps of Guilsborough, took over his father's private hire business after he died. During the war, the vehicle, a Chevrolet, was commandeered by the authorities, with two lorries with bus bodies being allocated to Heeps. He used these to transport prisoners of war from Sulby Camp, along with transporting army girls from local hostels. He also conveyed labourers and construction workers from Kingsthorpe to an aerodrome at Bitteswell which was still being built.

Samuel Kirton's Fosters Booth to Northampton service was reduced during the war, terminating at this time at the Plough Hotel, Bridge Street.

Harry Webster was another operator to gain a contract to transport prisoners of war from a camp at Boughton. Alongside this, a workers' bus was operated between Fosters Booth and Northampton.

In May 1940, York Bros. of Cogenhoe cancelled its tours and excursion programme, along with its Northampton to Great Yarmouth service. The company was successful in gaining a number of workers' contracts in the Northampton area, as well as the munitions factories in the Coventry area. They were also involved in transporting evacuees from Northampton. Numerous airfields were constructed around the local area. Yorks operated a number of contracts, transporting builders to these sites. The Northampton to Wollaston service was maintained during the war, with a good level of service being upheld.

Northampton Corporation Transport converted a number of single-deck buses to ambulances, driven by women volunteers. The Corporation also helped to transport evacuees around Northamptonshire. From 26 September, a number of off-peak services were cut due to fuel rationing, with peak time services operating unaffected. Twenty-nine stops on the network were removed. By 1941, many of the bus services were finishing at 9.30pm. London Transport lost a number of vehicles due to enemy action. Over 400 buses were loaned to the capital, with Northampton Corporation loaning five of its Guy FCX double-deckers. Part of the St James garage was rented to Armstrong Whitworth for aircraft production, with extra security measures put in place.

1946

After the war, the Wappenham to Northampton service held by Walter Lawrence was transferred to the Weston-by-Weeden to Northampton licence.

The summer of 1946 saw the Northampton to Great Yarmouth service operated by York Bros. recommence operation after its withdrawal during the war years.

The business of T.E. Haynes of Priors Marston was acquired by George Thomas Owen of Upper Boddington. By August, eleven licences had been applied for, including an express service between Upper Boddington and Northampton, operating on alternate Tuesdays and Saturdays.

1946 proved to be a busy year for Northampton Corporation Transport. At the beginning of the year the following services were operated: route 1 to Weston Favell; the 2 to Bush Hill; the 3 to Kingsland Avenue; 4 to Headlands; 5 to Five Bells; 6 to Abbots Way; 7 to Far Cotton; 8 to Kingsthorpe via Billing Road; route 9 to Kingsthorpe via St James; route 10 to Methyr Road; 11 to Manfield Hospital and the 12 to Warren Road. A new circular service, the 14, was introduced from 7 April. It ran from Regent Square via the Barracks College of Technology, School of Art, Northampton School for Girls, Racecourse Military Establishment, Randall Road, Kingsley Primary School, Kenmuir Avenue, Northampton Golf Club, Park Avenue North, Abington Park North, Abington Park, Wellingborough Road and Abington Square.

1946 also saw a set of co-ordinated services operated with United Counties, allowing the Corporation to extend services to Far Cotton (Queen Eleanor Cross/Gloucester Avenue), Bants Lane and North Western Avenue. In return, the fare protection between St James and Far Cotton was withdrawn. The protection on Kettering Road moved from The Avenue to the Golf House, whilst on Welford Road it moved from Kingsway to High Street, Kingsthorpe. The Far Cotton route extension started on 29 September, whilst routes 6 and 12 to Bants Lane and Dallington Park Road started on 1 December.

Other services were introduced in the final four months of the year. From 29 September route 16 commenced operation to Cranford Road, with the 18 starting up at the same time to Pleydell Road. Route 15 was introduced from 1 December, running to Headlands; whilst at the same time route 17 commenced running to Merthyr Avenue. Route 2 was re-routed along Stimpson Avenue in December, not being received well by the employees of the Manfield Shoe Factory on Wellingborough Road.

1947

Blakesley-based KW Services Limited applied to add extra journeys on Sundays to its Woodford to Northampton service, along with a daily service on the Eydon to Northampton route, the latter replacing the weekend-only service. Both were granted, starting from 5 May. May also saw the refinement of some of KW Services' routes. The Little Preston to Northampton route was absorbed into the Eydon to Northampton route. In October, a successful application was made to operate a Wednesday, Saturday and Sunday service between Moreton Pinkney, Adstone, Maidford, Litchborough, Bugbrooke and Kislingbury. A month later, the Woodend to Northampton service was withdrawn from Fosters Booth and Rothersthorpe. The village of Foxley was added to the Woodend–Litchborough–Northampton route, only to be taken away in November.

Billing Aquadrome, located on the edge of Northampton, proved to be a popular attraction in 1947 with both locals and those from further afield. York Bros. applied to the Traffic Commissioner in August to operate a Sunday only service between the site and Northampton, Market Square. In December, an application was made for a daily service. Both applications were met with objections from United Counties, but nonetheless were granted.

The Upper Boddington to Northampton express service operated by George Owen was altered to a stage-carriage service in 1947, running on Saturdays and alternate Tuesdays. The Northampton terminus at this time was located at Mayorhold.

The issue of co-ordination between Northampton Corporation Transport and United Counties has been mentioned already in this book, the former operator being more reluctant than the latter. This idea was supported by the Traffic Commissioners, but they had no power to enforce this. Northampton Corporation had the belief that they should have the rights to be the only operator within the Northampton Borough boundary. By the end of the war, housing estates had developed in Northampton beyond the bus termini served by Northampton Corporation. The two concerns met on 25 February 1946, with United Counties putting forward proposals with regards to the two pooling resources, these being rejected, with counter proposals being made. These involved little co-ordination on routes between the town centre and the south and west of Northampton. Further negotiations eventually resulted in a joint agreement whereby the protection of fares on London and Towcester roads, between the town centre and Forest Road and Queen Eleanor Road, along with the establishment of joint bus stops and common fares on both roads, came into existence. Northampton Corporation's route between Ashford's Corner and Queen Eleanor Cross, serving London Road, was extended from Rothersthorpe Road to Mere Way, located on the Towcester Road. All of these agreements came into existence on 29 September.

The next scheme saw the fare protection zone to the west of the town centre move to St James Square from the junction of Weedon Road/Duston Road and Harlestone Road/Warren Road; allowing United Counties to pick up more local passengers. To counterbalance this, Northampton Corporation extended their service from Abbots Way on Weedon Road to the junction of Duston Road/Bants Lane. The Warren Road service was extended to the Dallington Turn. Again, common fares and joint bus stops were introduced along these routes, coming into effect from 1 December. These two schemes operated for an initial three-month trial period.

After this, further co-ordination was reached. The restrictions between St James Square and the town centre imposed on United Counties were removed, with common bus stops and fares introduced. The protection zone on the Kettering Road services moved from the Bridle Path to the Golf House, this being one stop closer to Northampton town centre. Common bus stops were introduced on the route between the town centre and Manfield Hospital, United Counties still not being able to carry passengers between the town centre and Golf House. Northampton Corporation were given permission to introduce a new service between the town centre and North Western Avenue. In return, the protection zone on Welford Road moved from Kingsway to High Street, Kingsthorpe, common bus stops being introduced between this latter point and North Western Avenue.

Both the St James and Kettering Road schemes were to have been implemented from 30 November 1947, but opposition was met from the Union. This delayed the scheme, with joint stops on the Kettering Road never being introduced.

In addition to the above changes, Northampton Corporation introduced a new service, the 20, to Military Road from 27 April. From 14 April, the Corporation introduced special workings which connected to special trains during the summer, the popularity of these services meaning they had to be pre-booked. For this, a circular route was introduced running via Abington, Kingsley, Kingsthorpe and Far Cotton. From 10 August this service was joined by a new service operating to Bush Hill, running via Wellingborough Road. A compromise was reached with the Manfield Shoe Factory after route 2 had been diverted away from it in 1946. A new service, the 21, was introduced to serve the factory.

1948

Sidney Knight acquired the business of A.R. Surridge of Harpole in 1948. This expanded the excursions programme offered, operating these from both Northampton and Harpole.

KW Services Ltd applied for a licence to divert a single journey each way on its Woodend to Northampton service to operate via Blakesley, Foxley and Litchborough on Wednesdays and Saturdays. This had previously been operated by the company, being withdrawn in November 1947.

Little is known about the operations of W.B. Bartram & Sons (Flax Mill Coaches). Established in July 1948, this operator used a coach on staff transport to its mill on the east side of Northampton. British Timken Ltd was another local factory to purchase a bus to transport its staff from the local area to its factory in Duston.

In December, York Bros. were granted permission to operate double-deck buses on their Northampton to Billing Aquadrome service.

George Owen's Upper Boddington to Northampton service was extended to Chacombe. The alternate Tuesday service was withdrawn at this time, being replaced by a weekly Wednesday service.

1949

Following the death of Sidney Knight in the early part of 1949, his daughter, Mary Elizabeth Knight, took over the business from 4 February. In April she applied to the Traffic Commissioner for two excursion licences from Northampton and Harpole, as well as the Brixworth to Northampton stage carriage service.

1950–1959

1950

Harry Webster of Pattishall expanded his business during the first half of 1950, acquiring the business of two local operators. Francis Belgrove died in 1949, with his routes into Northampton passing to his daughters who continued to operate them until March 1950. It was at this time that they sold the business to Harry Dunnet of Wellingborough who soon sold it on to Webster. The second was the business of Kirton of Eastcote. This operator ceased operating his Northampton to Fosters Booth service from 29 April. The service ran via Milton Malsor, Gayton, Eastcote, Ascote and Pattishall. Webster took on the service from 1 May.

In November 1950, York Bros. was successful in applying for a short-term express licence to operate a workers' service between Northampton Market Square and the Whitfield AFV depot located near to Syresham, on Mondays to Fridays. This formed a contract for the Company that lasted until 1959.

1951

George Leonard Edwards was another independent to sell out to another local independent. Edwards sold his Paulerspury to Northampton service to Basford Coaches Limited who, in November, applied for a licence for the service. The route did not pass to Basford's until 3 February 1952. The new operator added a Tuesday service to the Wednesday, Saturday and Sunday operation. It was on 6 December 1950 that the operations of Arthur Basford became a limited company. In April 1951, an application was made under this name to operate the services unaltered. By this time, the Northampton terminus had changed to the yard of the Plough Hotel. Some journeys had also been extended past Greens Norton to Bradden.

1952

By 1952, Knights Luxury Coaches wished to dispose of their Brixworth to Northampton stage carriage service, focusing on tours and excursions. From 1 May 1952, the route was absorbed into United Counties' existing route 12 running between Northampton and Market Harborough. The Brixworth to Northampton service originated with J.H. Mills of Brixworth in 1924.

An application to the Traffic Commissioner was made by KW Services Limited in March to operate a service between Byfield, Woodford Halse, Preston Capes, Litchborough, Bugbrooke, Kislingbury and Northampton. This was granted.

1953

Further co-ordination between Northampton Corporation Transport and United Counties was made during 1953. By February, the Sunnyside housing estate, in north Northampton, became the subject. Negotiations commenced in 1950, with Northampton Corporation proposing to extend their existing Kingsthorpe Road service from the Five Bells terminus to the junction of Harborough Road/Chalcombe Avenue, as well as extending their service into the estate as it developed, making an eventual loop to Boughton Green Road and back to the Five Bells. The proposal was within the Borough boundary, and the Corporation thought that it was only right that they should be entitled to the passenger traffic generated.

At the same time, a service between Derngate bus station and Whitehills Estate was operated by United Counties. Protection for Northampton Corporation ran from the Royal Oak, just north of Five Bells. United Counties had the view that since they had been operating this route for a number of years, they were entitled to the benefits from the new estate.

Various proposals were put forward between 1950 and 1953, with both parties knowing that they had at some point to reach an agreement. It was eventually agreed that United Counties would not voice objections to Northampton Corporation serving the Sunnyside Estate, with the latter paying United Counties a fee of ½d per passenger for those picked up or set down after the Five Bells terminus.

From February, Northampton Corporation introduced two new routes, the 24 and 25. These replaced route 5, and were extended from Five Bells in Kingsthorpe to the Sunnyside Estate. It was also proposed that Northampton Corporation would extend route 21 to Cottarville, running via Booth Lane South and Ferndale Road. However, objections were met from the public and the service extension did not go ahead.

1954

A name associated with bus and coach operation not only in Northampton, but Northamptonshire, is Country Lion. Although the Company has had several owners, the roots can be traced back to 16 October 1954 when Lion Services (Northampton) Limited was formed by Keith Norman Coates. The first minibus entered the fleet in 1954, a second arriving in 1961. These were used on unknown contracts.

1955

In January 1955, Richardson Coaches of Hartwell started a relationship with Pianoforte Supplies Ltd of Roade. At this time, the Company won the contract for a service between the factory and Gayton. They applied for a second licence to operate a service between Guildhall Road, Northampton and the factory in Roade. The operation of this route is, however, unclear. At the same time the Company also applied for a licence to operate an express service between Northampton, Market Square, Kislingbury, Bugbrooke and the Cornhill Ballroom on a Saturday evening. This was duly granted.

1956

Basford Coaches' service between Bradden and Northampton was re-routed during May 1956 to serve Duncote, Caldecote and Tiffield. The Northampton terminus for the route was also altered at this time, moving from the Plough Hotel to Gas Street Car Park.

In August 1956, York Bros. applied to the Traffic Commissioner to amend the Northampton to Wollaston services. The alterations affected the route east of Grendon. They wished to run services alternately either via Easton Mauditt and Bozeat, or Wollaston and Bozeat, returning via Easton Mauditt. These alterations were granted in September, with the night service provision being withdrawn at this time.

1957

In April 1957, KW Services Limited withdrew its Wednesday only service from Eydon to Northampton. However, it was reinstated in September, whilst the Moreton Pinkney to Northampton service was withdrawn.

During 1957 Harry Webster gained contracts for the Plessey factory in Caswell. They ran between Campbell Square, Northampton and Kislingbury.

1958

March 1958 saw the three licences held by Basford Coaches Ltd for the Bradden to Northampton service combine onto a solitary licence.

York Bros. of Cogenhoe applied to the Traffic Commissioner in April 1958 to introduce a number of longer distance day tours to its portfolio, this being granted in May. Another application was made in October to reduce the Northampton to Great Yarmouth service to Saturday and Sunday operation only between Easter and Whitsun. This was also granted and commenced during the 1959 season.

Harry Webster of Pattishall expanded his operations further during 1958, when, on 1 June, he purchased the business of Samuel Walters of Helmdon. Two stage-carriage services were operated by Walters, one of which entered Northampton. This ran between Greatworth and Northampton, serving the villages of Culworth, Helmdon, Wappenham, Abthorpe, Towcester before using the A43 to reach Northampton. The service operated on Wednesdays, Saturdays and Sundays. It was soon curtailed back to Culworth before being cut back further to Helmdon. In September 1958, Harry Webster gained the school contract to carry students between Bugbrooke and Duston school.

During 1958, United Counties merged routes 128 (Northampton–Bedford) and the 149 (Bedford–Cambridge) to create a through service between Northampton, Bedford and Cambridge, this taking up route number 128. At the same time, United Counties introduced a new service between Northampton, Olney and Newport Pagnell, this new facility taking route number 129. Both routes commenced on 13 April.

The Thursday evening service between Wappenham and Northampton operated by Walter Lawrence was withdrawn in the autumn of 1958.

1959

On 30 August, United Counties revised and reshaped the routes operating on the Northampton–Kettering–Corby–Stamford corridor. The majority of changes affected the Corby and Kettering areas. However, route 256 was curtailed to operate between Northampton, Kettering and Corby only, operating hourly Sunday to Fridays, with a half-hourly service on Saturdays.

United Counties introduced a new local service in the Northampton area numbered 302. It ran between Northampton and Moulton, via Wellingborough Road and Booths Lane. A fifteen-minute frequency was achieved between Northampton and Buttocks Booth at this time, this being served by routes 256, 302, 329 and 401. The introduction of the 302 service restricted any possible extension by Northampton Corporation Transport routes radiating to the east of Northampton.

United Counties made use of the new M1 motorway in the summer of 1959 when duplicate services operated between Nottingham, Leicester, Northampton and London. This became one of the first coach services to use the newly opened motorway.

In 1959, the terminus of services operated by Basford Coaches Ltd moved once again, this time from Gas Street to The Mayorhold.

The majority of original horse-drawn trams operated by the Northampton Street Tramway Company in the 1880s and 1890s were double-decks. They could carry eighteen apiece on each deck. One of these tramcars is photographed on Kettering Road, Northampton. *Barry Cross Collection/Online Transport Archive*

Northampton Street Tramways Company operated a handful of single-deck horse-drawn tramcars. Number 3 represents the type, seen paused outside the St James Café. *John Meredith Collection/Online Transport Archive*

Tramcar 1 was the first of twenty electric tramcars purchased by Northampton Corporation Tramways to replace the fleet of horse-drawn trams. It is seen blinded for its journey to Kingsthorpe. *Barry Cross Collection/Online Transport Archive*

Similar tramcar 7 is captured by the camera heading down The Drapery, Northampton. Today the road houses a number of bus stops for services passing through and terminating/starting from The Drapery. *Barry Cross Collection/Online Transport Archive*

Kettering Road finds tramcar 13 which is photographed travelling towards Kingsley Park. *Barry Cross Collection/Online Transport Archive*

Car 15 is photographed heading towards Kingsley Park whilst travelling through St James End. *Barry Cross Collection/Online Transport Archive*

Tramcar 16 is captured on the other side of Northampton, at Kingsthorpe. It is being kept company by similar tram number 2. *Barry Cross Collection/Online Transport Archive*

Below is another view of tramcar 16 which is one of two photographed passing Abington Park. It is seen carrying a full load whilst bound for nearby Northamptonshire County Cricket Ground. *Barry Cross Collection/Online Transport Archive*

Tramcar 22 is captured by the camera in The Drapery whilst heading towards Kingsthorpe. Number 22 was new to the Corporation in 1905. *Barry Cross Collection/Online Transport Archive*

The final new tramcars to be taken into stock by Northampton Corporation Tramways were four single-deck English Electric saloon cars, arriving in 1922. Number 34 was numerically the first of the quartet and seen below. *Barry Cross Collection/Online Transport Archive*

BD2188 was a Maudslay double-deck purchased by George Henry Clarke of Weedon to operate a service between Daventry and Northampton. This fine double-decker is photographed above seen carrying a heavy load. *Roger Warwick Collection*

1913 saw Frank Beeden purchase a Napier charabanc (MX9742). He operated this along with his fleet of lorries from the yard of the Plough Hotel, located in Bridge Street. This charabanc is photographed alongside Beeden's collection of lorries. *Roger Warwick Collection*

William Alfred Nightingale commenced operation in 1920, running a route between Towcester and Northampton. He was based at the Wheatsheaf Hotel in Towcester, trading as The Wheatsheaf Motor Coach Service. NH4288 was a Dodson bodied Guy saloon, new to the company in July 1922. *Roger Warwick Collection*

The fleet of AECs operated by F&E Beeden of Northampton in 1923 can be seen in this photograph. Strachan bodied AEC NH4438 is the vehicle closest to the camera. *Roger Warwick Collection*

Formed in 1914, the Northampton Motor Omnibus Company Limited (NMOC) was one of the larger independent operators in Northampton, with forty-three vehicles being operated between 1914 and 1927. NH4819 was a Strachan & Brown bodied Daimler Y type, new to the company in March 1923. This vehicle passed to United Counties in June 1928, when the latter company purchased the NMOC. *Roger Warwick Collection*

One of the early motor buses operated by Northampton Corporation Tramways can be seen in this photograph taken outside All Saints' Church at the top end of The Drapery. *Barry Cross Collection/Online Transport Archive*

BD9105 was new to United Counties in April 1924, carrying body number C8. It is photographed blinded for route 2 to Wellingborough.
Roger Warwick Collection

XK7356 was another Daimler vehicle to be operated by the Northampton Motor Omnibus Company during the 1920s. This particular bus was new to the company in 1925 and was based on the Daimler CB chassis, carrying locally built Grose bodywork.
Roger Warwick Collection

September 1926 saw the first of two Studebaker saloons purchased by Nightingales. Registration mark NH7263 was carried by this vehicle, which has a Metcalfe twenty-seater coach body. *Roger Warwick Collection*

The Leyland Lion became the preferred choice of single-deck to be purchased by United Counties in the late 1920s. 108 (L11) – RP5007 was one of the first members of the type to operate with the Company. It is seen heading toward Northampton showing off its rear-entrance. *S.J. Butler Collection*

The first double-deck motorbuses arrived with Northampton Corporation Tramways in August 1928. By August 1929, ten Grose bodied Guy FCXs were in operation with the company, replacing trams on the Wellingborough Road route. 26 (NH8996) was new to the Corporation in March 1929. *S.J. Butler Collection*

The coach fleet of W.A. Nightingale had been upgraded by the late 1920s, early 1930s. VV498 was a Petty bodied Gilford 168OT coach, purchased by the company in March 1931 to operate the Northampton to London express service. It is posed next to the Queen Eleanor Cross in Northampton. *Roger Warwick Collection*

BVC268 was the first Daimler COG5 to operate with Northampton Corporation. It was new to Daimler in July 1936, acquired by the Corporation in the same month. Carrying a Strachan body, it was numbered 84 and used in comparison with a Leyland Titan TD4. The COG5 became the chosen model, with a number of the type being purchased by Northampton Corporation from 1937. *John Meredith Collection/Online Transport Archive*

1937 saw the Daimler COG5 replace the Crossley chassis for new vehicle orders for Northampton Corporation. 103 (VV7875) is seen operating route 9 to Northampton town centre. *J.S. Cockshott Archive*

Roe bodied Daimler COG5 106 (VV8202) was new to Northampton Transport in August 1939. It is seen heading towards Northampton town centre on route 8. *J.S. Cockshott Archive*

108 (VV8204) was one of the last Daimler COG5s to be delivered to Northampton Corporation Transport, as well as one of the last new buses to be purchased before the outbreak of the Second World War. It is photographed operating route 9 to Five Bells. *Phil Tatt/Online Transport Archive*

Billing Aquadrome became a popular destination for both those living in Northampton, as well as those who came from further afield. The aquadrome itself is located on the eastern edge of the town, outside of the area of operation of Northampton Corporation Transport. However, the vehicles operated on loan to Yorks Bros. Duple bodied Daimler CWD6 131 (VV8993), new to the Corporation in October 1945, is seen at Billing Aquadrome. *John Meredith/Online Transport Archive*

Northampton Corporation was amongst many operators in the country to loan buses to the London Passenger Transport Board during the war, replacing buses that had been damaged by enemy action. October 1940 saw four of the Corporation's Guy FCX double-decks go on loan to London. One of these was 27 (NH8997), photographed operating route 100 in East London. *S.J. Butler Collection*

Tilling bodied AEC Regent GW6292 was one of six of the type to be purchased by United Counties from sister company Brighton, Hove & District in 1943. It is seen travelling towards Stony Stratford via Roade. *S.J. Butler Collection*

Ten Roe bodied Crossley DD42/3s were purchased by Northampton Corporation to help with post-war fleet replacement. These arrived in November 1946 and are represented by 141 (VV9141), seen passing through Dallington whilst operating route 4 towards Broadmead Avenue. *John Meredith/Online Transport Archive*

153 (ANH153) was part of a batch of twenty NCB bodied Daimler CVG6 double-deckers to be taken into stock by Northampton Corporation during 1947. It is seen heading towards the Five Bells on route 8. *J.S. Cockshott Archive*

Northampton's Market Square provides the backdrop to 175 and 176 (ANH175/6). This pair of Roe bodied Daimler CVG6s were new to Northampton Corporation in May 1949. *J.S. Cockshott Archive*

Ten Roe bodied Daimler CVG6s were taken into stock by Northampton Corporation Transport during March 1950. 181 (ANH181) is numerically the second of the batch and is seen operating route 16 towards Cranford Road. *Phil Tatt/Online Transport Archive*

Two Burlingham bodied Leyland Tiger TS7s arrived with York Bros. in March 1950. The first of the pair, FNV700, is seen in the yard of Yorks Bros. *J.S. Cockshott Archive*

Twenty-one ECW bodied Bristol KSW6B double-decks were delivered to United Counties during 1952. 700 (CNH700) is seen approaching Derngate returning from its trip to East Northamptonshire. *J.S. Cockshott Archive*

In 1952, a fleet of ECW bodied Bristol LWL6B saloons entered the United Counties fleet. 860 (CNH860) is again seen approaching Derngate. *J.S. Cockshott Archive*

In May 1952, the Midland area of the Eastern National Omnibus Company transferred to the control of United Counties, adding garages in Bedford, Biggleswade, Huntingdon and Aylesbury. With the acquisition came eighty-nine ECW bodied Bristol K5Gs. 726 (MPU10) represents this large batch. *J.S. Cockshott Archive*

March 1953 saw the arrival of Burlingham Seagull coaches with Yorks, one carrying an AEC Regal chassis, the other a Leyland Royal Tiger chassis. JBD100 carried the latter chassis and is captured by the camera whilst operating a private hire. *794 Preservation Group*

By 1954, the Bristol chassis had changed to the LD6B model, again carrying ECW bodywork. ORP30 was new to United Counties in September 1957, taking rolling stock number 530. *J.S. Cockshott Archive*

LRP700 was one of two Duple Elizabethan bodied Leyland Tiger Cubs to be delivered to York Bros. in June 1955. It remained operational with the company until October 1963. *794 Preservation Group*

A pair of Craven bodied AEC Regent IIIs were acquired by Yorks Bros. from Birds of Stratford-upon-Avon in November and December 1956, originating with London Transport. KGK736 was first to arrive, new as RT1477, and took rolling stock number 4 with its new owner. *J.S. Cockshott Archive*

York Bros. took stock of a trio of Duple Britannia bodied AEC Reliance coaches in 1959. The first, TBD1, arrived with the company in March and is seen below. *794 Preservation Group*

TBD2 was one of the other pair of AEC Reliance/Duple Britannia coaches delivered to Yorks Bros. in May 1959. It took up rolling stock number 73 with the company. *794 Preservation Group*

Black & White jointly operated the Associated Motorways service to Cheltenham. SAD189 is photographed blinded for its return journey inside Northampton garage. *J.S. Cockshott Archive*

For a number of years, Wesley's of Stoke Goldington operated a service between Stoke Goldington, Newport Pagnell and Northampton. The fleet is represented here by 372BBH, a Duple bodied Commer Avenger IV, new to the company in April 1957. *794 Preservation Group*

Duple Britannia bodied AEC Reliance 75 (VBD75) arrived with York Bros. in January 1960. This smart vehicle was one of four AEC Reliance coaches delivered to York Bros. during 1960. *J.S. Cockshott Archive*

The **1961** deliveries of Daimler CVG6s arrived in February. 223 (MNH223) was the second member of the batch. *794 Preservation Group*

Three Duple Britannia bodied AEC Reliance coaches, two of which arrived in April. YBD79 was one of these and was displayed at the UK Coach Rally in Brighton during 1961. *794 Preservation Group*

June 1962 saw the arrival of 84BNV, a Duple Northern Continental bodied AEC Reliance coach with York Bros. It remained operational with the company until April 1968 when it was sold for further use. *794 Preservation Group*

The Daimler CVG6 double-deck became a familiar sight in Northampton, becoming the standard double-deck model operated by Northampton Corporation since 1947, originally bodied by Northern Coach Builders before changing to Roe bodywork in 1953. The style changed in 1957 to that seen below. 248 (BNH248C) represents the type and is seen passing All Saints' Church in The Drapery whilst operating route 14. *794 Preservation Group*

Daimler Fleetline saloons were used to convert routes 2, 8, 10, 17 and 21 to single-deck one-person operated buses. 19 (UNH19L) is seen shortly after arrival with Northampton Corporation. *Laurence Knight*

In 1977 and 1978, thirty-six Alexander bodied Bristol VRTs were purchased by Northampton Corporation. 35 (PBD35R) was the first of these, arriving in May 1977. It is seen on Abington Street heading towards the Five Bells on route 8. *Laurence Knight*

43 (PBD43R) was another Alexander bodied Bristol VRT delivered to Northampton Corporation in May 1977. It is seen heading towards Headlands on route 15. *794 Preservation Group*

Geoff Amos of Eydon, near Daventry, operated several routes into Northampton. These mostly ran between the two towns, serving local villages on their journey. The fleet is represented here by RBD405R, a Willowbrook bodied Bedford YMT new to the company in October 1976. *794 Preservation Group*

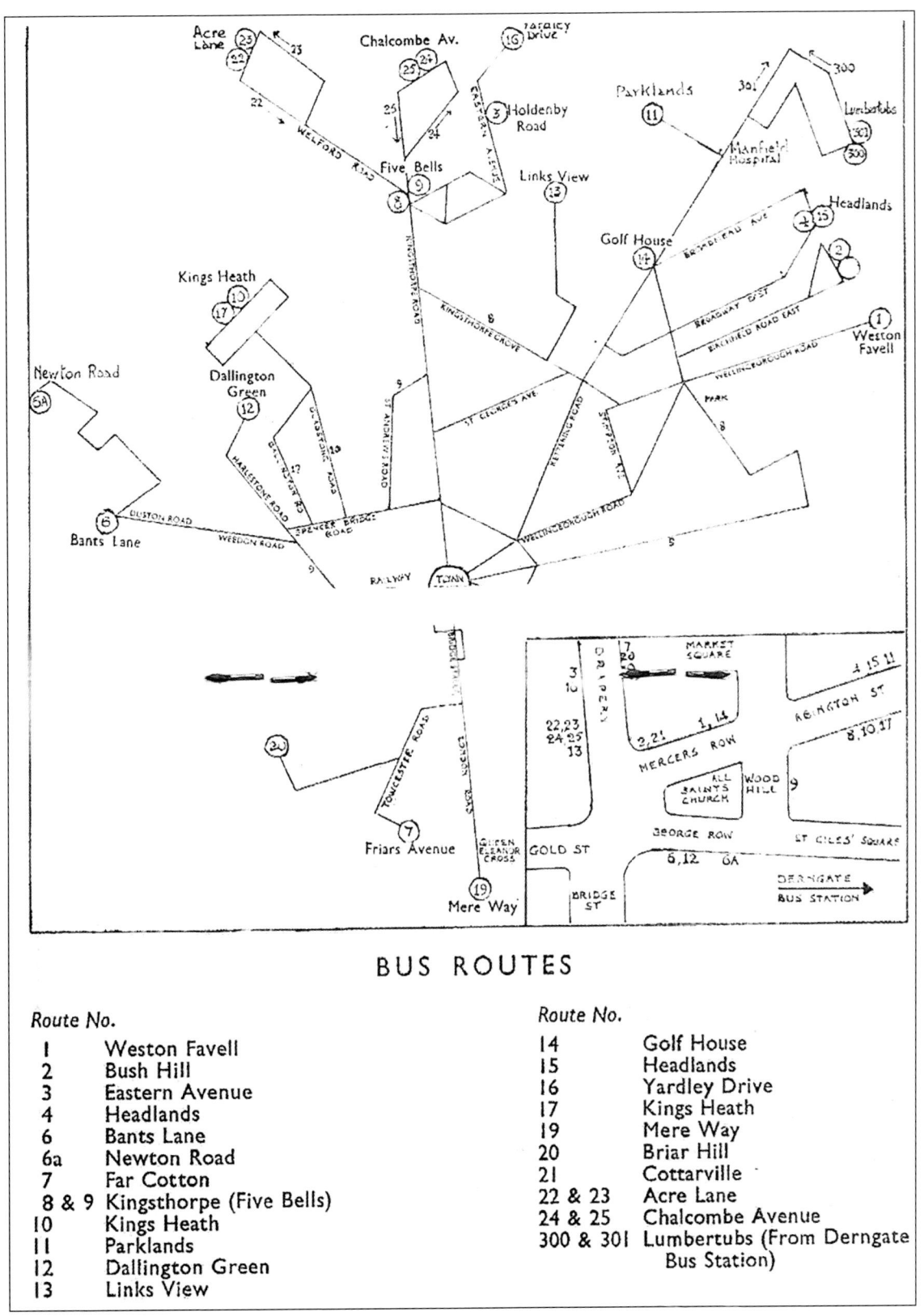

BUS ROUTES

Route No.		Route No.	
1	Weston Favell	14	Golf House
2	Bush Hill	15	Headlands
3	Eastern Avenue	16	Yardley Drive
4	Headlands	17	Kings Heath
6	Bants Lane	19	Mere Way
6a	Newton Road	20	Briar Hill
7	Far Cotton	21	Cottarville
8 & 9	Kingsthorpe (Five Bells)	22 & 23	Acre Lane
10	Kings Heath	24 & 25	Chalcombe Avenue
11	Parklands	300 & 301	Lumbertubs (From Derngate Bus Station)
12	Dallington Green		
13	Links View		

A map showing the routes operated by Northampton Corporation Transport, taken from the April 1973 timetable booklet. *794 Preservation Group*

1960–1969

1960

1960 was the final year of operation for Knights Luxury Coaches. Talks were entered into with Yorks Bros. of Cogenhoe, Knight's main competitor on excursions and tours from Northampton. An agreement was reached in February, at which time the business was purchased by Yorks. The licences for the tours and excursions from Harpole and Northampton were granted in May and June 1960. The sale was officially completed on 1 July.

The 6A was a new route introduced on 16 October, jointly operated by Northampton Corporation Transport and United Counties. The service ran between Northampton town centre and Cotswold Avenue, located on the Bants Lane Estate. However, United Counties did not take up their share of the service. The route provided a link to both Express Lifts and British Timken.

1961

Richardson Coaches of Hartwell had established a Saturday evening service between Northampton, Market Square and Cornhill Ballroom in 1955. The licence for this service came up for renewal in February 1961. At this time United Counties voiced some objections to the renewal, resulting in it being rejected by the Traffic Commissioner.

In June 1961, Ted Johnson, a friend of Walter Lawrence, purchased his business. Johnson soon applied for three of Lawrence's licences, including the Weston-by-Weedon to Northampton service. However, Johnson was based in Hanslope, a considerable distance from Wappenham. Arrangements were made with Jack Jeffs of Helmdon to take over the services. Jeffs made an application to the Traffic Commissioner in November 1962 to acquire Johnson's licences, these being granted on 1 March 1963.

The long-established service between Birmingham, Northampton and Lowestoft, jointly worked with Midland Red and Eastern Counties, was operated solely by United Counties as the X3. The Birmingham leg of the route was cut, and the new X3 operated between Northampton and Lowestoft on summer Saturdays.

A new feeder service was introduced between Corby and Northampton during 1961 to connect with the Nottingham to London express service.

1962

1962 saw the journeys on United Counties X1 (Nottingham–London) that used the M1 motorway renumbered to the M1. During the year, a second feeder service was also introduced between Irthlingborough and Northampton, linking with the London to Nottingham express service.

The closure of the Northampton to Bedford rail line led to a number of limited-stop journeys being introduced on the 128 service, these running twelve minutes faster than the full 128 route.

The years before 1962 had seen the New Duston area of Northampton expand considerably. To provide bus services to the area, United Counties extended route 321 (Derngate–Quarry Road) to Northfield Road and Woodland Close to provide a regular service. This was the only town service to be operated by United Counties at this time. A second was introduced from 24 June. The 323 ran between Northampton and Harlestone, incorporating some journeys previously operated by the 321. It served St Crispin's Hospital and Upper Harlestone village.

1963

United Counties introduced service revisions within the Northampton area from 13 January, taking out mileage from the Sunday timetable. Further revisions were implemented from 7 July, at which time all departures from Derngate bus station departed from the standard departure bays for individual services. From this date the 344 (Northampton–Wappenham) was also withdrawn.

In 1963, Lion Services (Northampton) Ltd applied to the Traffic Commissioner to operate six circular services centred on Northampton, operating out into the Northamptonshire countryside. The proposed routes were to serve a number of villages, along with Market Harborough, Wellingborough and Old Stratford. Such was the area that Lion Services was intending to cover with these six services, it was no surprise that the routes were met with opposition from United Counties and Northampton Corporation, along with Midland Red, Basford Coaches of Greens Norton, Johnsons Coaches of Hanslope and Websters Coaches of Pattishall.

In addition to these services, Lion Services (Northampton) Ltd submitted an additional application to run a workers' only service for Avon Cosmetics between their site in Nunn Mills Road to St Giles Street. Northampton Corporation Transport voiced their objections as they operated a service to nearby Midsummer Meadow.

1964

January 1964 saw the express network of services renumbered by United Counties. The Nottingham–Leicester–Northampton–London M1 service was renumbered the MX5. Duplicate services between Nottingham, Leicester and London did not call at Northampton and these journeys were numbered MX1. Later in the year, the MX1 developed into a full route of its own. The X1 between Northampton and London was renumbered the X6. The feeder services from Daventry, Corby and Irthlingborough to Northampton were also numbered the X1, X2 and X3. Friday and Sunday journeys were introduced on the MX6 between Northampton and London which were diverted to operate via Olney, Newport Pagnell and Woburn before using the M1 motorway, this commencing operation on 4 October 1963.

The coastal express services were also renumbered by United Counties. The Nottingham–Brighton/Eastbourne/Hastings services of the X2 were renumbered MX7. The X7 became a feeder service from Northampton to Toddington Service Centre on the M1 in Bedfordshire, serving Newport Pagnell and Woburn on its way.

The Northamptonshire services to Skegness, Great Yarmouth, Lowestoft, Clacton and Whipsnade Zoo took up route numbers X11/X12/X13/X14 and X19.

In March, Jeffs Coaches extended one journey on Saturdays on their Weston-by-Weedon to Northampton service to serve Culworth and Sulgrave. The Northampton terminus for this solitary service also moved from the Plough Hotel to Victoria Gardens. The Sunday service on the standard route was withdrawn from this date.

The six circular minibus services proposed by Lion Services (Northampton) Limited in 1963 saw the Traffic Commissioner visit Northampton in January 1964. It may be recalled that a number of operators objected to these six services. A decision was finally made in June 1964, the Traffic Commissioner refusing to grant these licences. However, the company was successful in gaining a licence in July for the workers' only service to Avon Cosmetics. The only alteration was the proposed terminus in St Giles Street was moved to Derngate.

Two new express services were introduced in 1964 by Premier Travel of Cambridge, linking the city with Lancashire. The first was numbered 77 and ran between Cambridge and Blackburn, whilst the second was numbered 78 and terminated in Blackpool. Both routes served Bedford, Northampton, Leicester and Birmingham, and provided a faster link between Cambridge and Birmingham than route 5. The introduction of these services created a frequency reduction on route 5.

On 6 June 1964, United Counties introduced a new express service, the MX8. It operated between Nottingham, Northampton, London and Margate/Ramsgate. A feeder service numbered X8 was also introduced operating between Northampton and Toddington Service Station. The service was introduced and operated jointly with the East Kent Road Car Co. Ltd.

United Counties route 324 (Northampton–Newport Pagnell) was extended in 1964 to Bletchley, providing the first direct bus service between these towns.

United Counties introduced a new route in 1964, the 403. This ran between Northampton, Wellingborough and Rushden before continuing on to Raunds. Route 404 also ran over a similar route, servicing the village of Irchester between Wellingborough and Rushden.

The Northampton–Wellingborough–Peterborough branch line was another railway line to close, doing so in May 1964. This led to the introduction of route 409 which was jointly operated with Eastern Counties between these locations.

1965

On 17 January 1965, United Counties route 302 was extended in the village of Moulton to terminate at Tarant Way. January also saw the extension of the M1 express northwards to Leicester. In this year an agreement was reached that express service MX4 would be jointly operated by United Counties, Trent and Midland General. The service operated from Alfreton to London via Derby, Loughborough, Leicester and Northampton. The route was marketed under the 'Derbyshire Express' name, this being carried on a board in the front screen of the coach.

The Wednesday only service between Chacombe, Upper Boddington and Northampton operated by George Owen was discontinued in June 1965.

1966

The single Saturday journey between Sulgrave and Northampton operated by Jeffs Coaches was curtailed in February to the original Weston-by-Weedon terminus. The route was also cut from four to three journeys on a Saturday.

Less than a year after the Wednesday service on the Chacombe, Upper Boddington and Northampton service operated by George Owen ceased, the Saturday operation on the same route came to an end, this taking place in March.

Country Lion Minibuses and name was sold by My Coates to Palmerston Garage (Northampton) Ltd in October. Six minibuses were acquired at this time. At the time of takeover, Lion Services, the previous owner, had been operating a contract for Avon Cosmetics, operating between Derngate and Nunn Mills Road. The new owners applied to continue operating this service.

Little happened during 1966 in relation to United Counties services in the Northampton area. The Northampton to New Duston service was renumbered, with the 321 operating to Quarry Road. Journeys to Woodland Close were numbered 322. This latter number was in use by a service between Northampton and Whilton Locks, which was renumbered 328 to accommodate the changes.

1967

Jeffs Coaches' stage-carriage service between Weston-by-Weedon and Northampton was again subject to a couple of changes during May 1967. The Western terminus was extended to Moreton Pinkney. In August the Northampton terminus moved from Victoria Gardens to Mayorhold.

Midland Red diverted route X96 from 2 September 1967 to operate via the Meriden bypass, allowing it to serve Oakengates. From this date, the route became a limited-stop service between Coventry and Wolverhampton.

United Counties route 310 (Northampton–Harpole) was split between new routes 310 and 311, both of which operated between Northampton and Daventry.

1968

United Counties local services 321 and 322 were revised in the Duston area to run in a circular fashion. They ran from their respective termini (Quarry Road–321 or Woodland Road–322) via Harlestone Road.

The Midland Red Bus Company had operated several services into Northampton from Banbury, Leicester and Shrewsbury since 1929. They had been using the Mayorhold as the terminus for these services. However, an agreement was reached between United Counties and Midland Red in 1968 for the latter company to use the Derngate Coach Station as their terminus. The latter company had been using Mayorhold up to this date.

On 11 August 1968 there was an extensive revision of United Counties services in the Northampton area. From this date, the 325 (Northampton–Roade–Potterspury–Stony Stratford) and 326 (Northampton–Roade–Hanslope–Wolverton) services were made into circular routes. These operated from Northampton via Roade, Stony Stratford, Roade and Northampton. The 330 operated anticlockwise from Roade to Potterspury,

Stony Stratford, Wolverton, Hanslope and Roade, with the 331 operating in a clockwise direction of the same route.

Changes were also made at this time to the Northampton to Towcester routes. The 340 (Northampton–Towcester–Paulerspury–Silverstone) and 342 (Northampton–Shutlanger–Paulerspury–Whittlebury) were both withdrawn. Parts of each service were amalgamated into new service 344 which ran between Northampton, Towcester, Paulerspury, Whittlebury and Silverstone. The 343 (Northampton and Gayton) lost its Sunday service, whilst the 345 (Northampton–Towcester–Silverstone) was revised, no longer serving Syresham after this date.

Under this scheme, most other United Counties services in the Northampton area were revised including the 312 and 316 Northampton to Market Harborough services.

1969

Jeffs Coaches acquired the business of Harry Webster in May 1969. Included in the sale was a service between Helmdon and Northampton. Jeff's existing Northampton service was altered to accommodate this. The Moreton Pinkney to Northampton service was truncated at this time to Helmdon.

On 18 May, United Counties withdrew its MX6 express service. The route had operated between Northampton, Olney and London, using the M1 Motorway between the latter two locations.

1970–1979

1970

John Herbert Sherrat of Corby applied for a licence in December 1970 to convey workers from Corby and other points across Northamptonshire to the Mettoy Co. Ltd factory in Northampton. The service had operated for a number of years prior to the application, the licence being duly granted in 1971.

The terminus for Jeffs Coaches' Helmdon to Northampton service moved from Mayorhold to St Johns Street during 1970.

British Timken Limited ceased operating its own staff transport for sports and social events. After this time the work passed to other operators.

During the year, United Counties reduced its Sunday service on route 401 (Northampton–Sywell–Wellingborough).

1971

The roads in Northampton town centre underwent redevelopment during 1971. As a result, the Mayorhold area could no longer be used as a terminus. A new terminus was set up in St Johns Street, this being used by a number of independent operators.

The issue of co-ordination between United Counties and Northampton Corporation raised its head again in the early 1970s with the growth of Northampton in the Eastern District. It was agreed that services to this new area of Northampton would be developed jointly between the two companies, with each operator being entitled to 50 per cent of the new service mileage and revenue. The first route was introduced on 29 March 1971 when route 300 came into operation. It operated from Derngate Bus Station via Kettering Road to the new Lumbertubs Estate, operating an hourly frequency on Mondays to Saturdays.

1973

From 8 January 1973, United Counties diverted a number of services to serve two industrial estates, on either side of the town. Routes 329 and 303 served Moulton Park Industrial Estate, the latter being a variant of the 302. A lunch time facility was provided, running via St Gregory's Road and Lumbertubs Way. Routes 321, 322 and 306 were diverted to serve the Lodge Farm Industrial Estate.

A breakthrough was made in 1973 in relation to the co-ordinated route operation between United Counties and Northampton Corporation. From 18 February, route

300, introduced the previous year, was revised and extended to run from St Gregory's Road, via Lumbertubs Way and Lumbertubs Lane to Kettering Road, before returning to Northampton town centre. A reverse service was also introduced, numbered 301. It was from this date that the route became jointly operated by United Counties and Northampton Corporation, the latter company entering Derngate bus station for the first time on a scheduled service. From 22 July, the route also served Tonmead Road, Penistone Road and Billing Brook Road. Northampton Corporation used one-person-operated single-deckers on the route, the first of many to operate with the Corporation.

In April, a group called the Central Activities Group was set up by the National Bus Company (NBC). Their main objective was to integrate and develop the coaching operations of the various NBC subsidiaries. From 1 October 1973, they became responsible for the nationwide express network, giving birth to National Express. It had been stipulated by the NBC that all coaches operating express work should be painted white. From this time the Nottingham–Leicester–Northampton–London services MX1, MX5 as well as the X1, X2, X3 and X6 services were transferred to the control of National Express. These services were renumbered 550, 555, 551, 552, 553 and 556 by National Express, but were still operated on the United Counties licence.

The Nottingham–Leicester–Northampton–London service operated by United Counties was added to the National Express network. It was integrated with local services, providing a two-hourly express service numbered X61, the same number used by Midland Red for their Leicester to Northampton service.

1974

United Counties introduced a number of service changes within Northamptonshire from 28 April. This included the renumbering of some services to free up numbers 300 to 310 for use on the Northampton Eastern District services. From this date the following services were affected:

305 Northampton–Nether Heyford–Daventry to 345
306 Northampton–Long Buckby–West Haddon to 346
308 Northampton–Long Buckby–Daventry to 348
310/1 Northampton–Weedon–Daventry to 340/1
312 Northampton–Brixworth–Market Harborough to 324
316 Northampton–Guilsborough–Market Harborough to 326
324 Northampton–Newport Pagnell–Bletchley to 332
328 Northampton–Whilton to 323
329 Northampton–Old to 339
343 Northampton–Gayton to 333
344 Northampton–Silverstone to 334
345 Northampton–Towcester–Syresham to 335
346 Northampton–Aylesbury to 336

Soon after this renumbering took place, a new service, the 304, was introduced in Northampton. Serving the Eastern District, it left the town centre along Wellingborough Road and ran via Standens Barn, Billing Brook Road, Birds Hill Road, Lings Way and Hayeswood Road, terminating at Brookside. Just before this service started on 11 March, the 305 was introduced linking King's Heath with Moulton Park Industrial Estate and Standens Barn.

Further service revisions came into effect from 20 October, some of which affected the Northampton area. Under these revisions, a number of peak-hour journeys, as well as Saturday and Sunday journeys, were withdrawn on a number of routes. However, another two town services were introduced during 1974. The 306 operated between Northampton town centre, Churchill Avenue and Weston Favell Centre; whilst the 307 ran between the town centre, Weston Favell Centre and Bellinge. These were both jointly operated by United Counties and Northampton Corporation. When the 307 commenced operation, roads in Bellinge were not completed, leading to the service temporarily terminating at Standens Barn until they were completed.

Ten years after it had been introduced, the 409 (Northampton–Thrapston) was withdrawn from 18 October. This had been one of the services introduced after the Northampton to Peterborough branch line closed in 1964.

In March, Midland Red withdrew the Coventry to Northampton section of route X96. From this date the route was replaced by two similar services, the 595 and 594. The latter route had originally operated between Rugby and West Haddon, with some journeys being extended to Northampton from this date.

1975

Palmerston Garage (Northampton) Ltd, trading as Country Lion, were successful in gaining a number of contracts for special needs student and adult transport by 1975, transporting them to places of education or work within the Northampton area.

A jointly operated service between Oxford, Bicester, Brackley, Towcester and Northampton was introduced on 18 May. Numbered 338, the route was operated by United Counties, Oxford-South Midland and Midland Red, each operating two return journeys on weekdays, and one on Sundays. The main aim of the route was to provide both local and national links at Oxford, Brackley and Northampton. Midland Red's 512 service between Banbury and Northampton was curtailed to Brackley, where it connected with the 338.

The Wellingborough area service revisions in July also saw alterations to the 402 to 406 group of services between Northampton, Wellingborough, Irthlingborough/Rushden and Raunds. A half-hourly provision was provided, with one journey per hour operating as the 404 to Raunds, with the other as the 403 to Rushden, via the Melloway Estate in the latter town. The 402 was withdrawn, being replaced by a shorter service between Wellingborough and Irthlingborough.

York Bros. of Cogenhoe sold its Northampton to Wollaston service to United Counties in 1975. From 31 August 1975, United Counties introduced two new services over this route. The first was numbered 363 which ran from Northampton, via Billing Road, Favell Green, Weston Favell Centre, Cogenhoe, Grendon and Wollaston. This route almost followed the traditional Yorks Bros. route with the addition of serving the Bellinge Estate and Weston Favell Centre. The second service was numbered 364 and operated directly between the two locations, not serving the Weston Favell Centre.

1976

As was mentioned in the introduction, Greyfriars Bus Station opened in April 1976, providing a central terminus for both Northampton Corporation and United Counties buses, along with a number of independent operators.

The withdrawal of significant financial support from Northamptonshire County Council led to a number of service reductions on the United Counties network across the county, affecting a number of country services entering Northampton. From 28 March, changes were made to services in the north-west of the county. Route 324 (Northampton–Market Harborough) was reduced north of Brixworth, whilst the 326 running between the same two locations was curtailed at Welford. At the same time, services were affected in the Daventry and Long Buckby areas. The 346 (Northampton–Long Buckby–West Haddon) service was curtailed at Long Buckby, after which it continued to Daventry, replacing route 348. The Bedford to Northampton service, route 128, lost the limited-stop facility.

Northampton town service 305 (Kings Heath–Moulton Park–Standens Barn) had the majority of its journeys extended to Bellinge. The Sunday provision on route 302 between Northampton and Moulton was withdrawn at this time, some of which were covered by route 401.

On 2 May local circular service 301 (Town Centre–Kettering Road–Billing Brook Road) was withdrawn. The shortfall was taken up by the 300 to Thorplands, this operating via Wellingborough Road. The loss of the 301 was also covered by Northampton Corporation's route 3.

The next round of service changes was introduced on 20 June, aiming to reduce the number of loss making services. This affected services on the Northampton, Kettering and Corby corridors. The services affected were:

254 (Northampton–Sywell–Kettering–Geddington–Corby)
255 (Northampton–Moulton–Walgrave–Kettering–Geddington–Corby)
256 (Northampton–Main Road–Kettering–Geddington–Corby).

1977

United Counties enhanced the service provision to the newly developed Eastern District from 27 March when a number of new services along with the extension of existing routes were implemented. Firstly, the 300 (Bus Station–Thorplands) was extended to Blackthorn via Brookside Centre, Tanners public house and Crestwood Road. The number 301 was reused for a new service which provided a connection from Greyfriars bus station to Blackthorn, running via Wellingborough Road, Weston Favell Centre, Brookside Centre, Hayeswood Road. The 304 had previously operated to Blackthorn, but from this date was diverted via Thorplands and Southfields to serve the Moulton Park Industrial Estate. The Kings Heath to Bellinge service 305 was revised in conjunction with the 304. The 306 service between Northampton and Weston Favell was reduced with alternative facilities to Lumbertubs and St Gregory's Road being provided by new service 307. This latter service ran from the Bus Station to Ecton Brook via Wellingborough Road, Booth Lane, St Gregory's Road, Weston Favell Centre, Standens Barn and Bellinge. Service 308 was introduced to operate to the British Timken factory in Duston from the various estates in the eastern area of the town. Finally, at the same time, the 302 (Northampton–Moulton) and the 329 (Northampton–Old) were co-ordinated to provide a better service along the route.

Services in the Duston area of Northampton were also revised in 1976. Route 321 was withdrawn, whilst services operating via Lodge Farm Industrial Estate were also withdrawn. All journeys were placed under route 322 which ran in the Duston area via Eastfield Road, Northfield Road, Firsview Drive and Harlestone Road to the Quarry Road terminus, returning along Main Road, Duston.

From 27 March 1977, a through service was reintroduced between Northampton and Aylesbury on routes 336 and 337.

1978

March 1978 saw the acquisition of Overstone Coaches of Sywell by Palmerston Garage (Northampton) Ltd (Country Lion). The latter company took on the contracts and private hires operated by Overstone Coaches.

For a third year in a row, funding was cut by Northamptonshire County Council, resulting in changes to a number of United Counties services in the county, this taking effect from 2 April. Routes between Northampton, Kettering and Corby were again affected by the changes. The basic frequency that had been provided between these locations was retained. Some journeys were diverted to serve the villages of Overstone and Sywell, covering parts of the 401, with others diverted to serve Cransley covering the loss of the 250. The replacement services were the 254 which ran between Northampton, Sywell, Kettering and Corby: the 255 (Northampton–Walgrave–Kettering–Corby). The route between Northampton, Main Road, Kettering and Corby was numbered 256.

Changes were also made to Northampton town services. Routes 300 and 301 (Northampton–Blackthorn Estate) had their evening and Sunday service reduced and replaced by new circular services 309, 310 and 311 (Bus Station–Weston Favell–Bellinge–Southfields). The 304 (Northampton–Southfields–Moulton Park) was also revised, the evening and Sunday services also being replaced by the 309 and 311. Routes 309/310/311 also replaced the evening and Sunday journeys on route 307 (Northampton–Bellinge–Ecton Brook). The frequency on route 305 (Northampton–Kings Heath) was also reduced at this time. Route 308 was extended from its terminus at British Timken to serve Southfields.

A number of country services were also affected. The Northampton to Earls Barton section of route 401 was transferred to new services 316 and 317, along with diversions of route 254 mentioned above. The Wellingborough to Earls Barton section was covered by a new route numbered 299. The 316 and 317 operated between Northampton, Moulton, Overstone, Sywell, Mears Ashby and Earls Barton. Service on the 318 and 319 (Northampton–Moulton–Walgrave–Old) was reduced, with timings between Northampton and Moulton being covered by the two new services. Route 323 (Northampton–Whilton) had its Wednesday service extended to Daventry, whilst the Saturday provision was withdrawn and replaced by new service 343 (Northampton–Harpole–The Brington). The 324/5/6 (Northampton–Market Harborough) group of services were consolidated into new services, providing more efficient operation of the routes using a single vehicle. The Northampton to Milton Keynes group of services (330/1/4) were reduced, but a half hourly service between Northampton, Hardingstone and Wootton was maintained. The Sunday service south of Roade was lost on these routes. A new route, the 339, was introduced to provide a late night facility on the London and Towcester Roads out of Northampton. Routes 340/1/2 (Northampton–Weedon–Daventry) were reduced from half-hourly to hourly. The service was increased into the Southbrook Estate in Daventry, replacing town services 350 and 351. The 345 (Northampton–Nether Heyford–Daventry) had some journeys diverted via Upper Heyford. A new Saturday shoppers service was introduced between Northampton, Newnham, Badby and Staverton via Daventry, operating alongside the 323. Service 346 (Northampton–Long Buckby–Daventry) had its timetable modified and reduced. The service was withdrawn from the village of Holdenby. Routes 363 and 364 (Northampton–Wollaston) were extended to Wellingborough, replacing service 415 between Bozeat and Wellingborough. Again, the Sunday service on these routes was withdrawn, with a reduction being made to the weekday and Saturday service. The 402-6 group of services between Northampton, Wellingborough, Irthlingborough/Rushden and Raunds was revised, with some being extended to Thrapston. Diversions within Higham Ferrers were made, replacing some local routes. These services were renumbered 292 to 296.

In April, several alterations were made to Midland Red's services between Coventry and Northampton. From this time, the 595 was withdrawn between the two locations. It was replaced by a new service, the 596. The route connected Coventry and Northampton, running via Brandon, Wolston, Rugby, West Haddon and Long Buckby.

1979

Country Lion moved from their Palmerston Road, Denmark Road and Victoria Road premises to a larger site at the St James Mill Road Industrial Estate. At this time, the Palmerston Road site was compulsorily purchased by Northampton Borough Council for redevelopment.

On 1 April 1979, Jeffs Coaches of Helmdon took over the services and vehicles of Basford's Coaches Ltd. The latter Company operated two stage-carriage services, both of which were based on Greens Norton. One of these ran to Northampton, operating on Mondays to Saturdays.

In 1979 there were further changes made to United Counties services. Routes 316 to 319 (Northampton–Moulton–Earls Barton/Old); 324-6 between Northampton, Brixworth and Market Harborough; or Northampton and Welford; 332 Northampton to Horton Gates; 333/5 Northampton–Towcester–Silverstone; 340-2 Northampton–Daventry; 345 Northampton–Nether Heyford–Daventry and 346 Northampton–Long Buckby–Daventry/West Haddon, which was renumbered 595, the same number which was used by Midland Red. The 330 and 331 services between Northampton and Milton Keynes were extended to Bletchley. All this took place on 15 July.

1980–1989

1980

Jeffs Coaches of Helmdon had inherited two stage-carriage services from Basford Coaches when this business was acquired on 1 April 1979. Soon after acquisition, Jeffs were keen to dispose of these and during the same year they approached United Counties. It was planned that the latter operator should take over operation of the services to Northampton from both Greens Norton and Helmdon on 30 August, but a strike at United Counties' Northampton garage at this time led to a three-week delay.

During 1980, United Counties routes 330/1 (Northampton–Milton Keynes) and 332 (Northampton–Horton Gates) saw a reduction in peak time and evening service.

After a number of years, discussions between Northamptonshire County Council, Northampton Borough Council's Transport Department and United Counties regarding a rational operation of services within Northampton Borough led to the signing of a tripartite agreement known as the Agency Agreement. This was signed on 19 February 1980, coming into effect from 2 March. Under the 1978 Transport Act, the aforementioned parties were given the power and duty to co-operate with each other to co-ordinate public transport. This Act gave Northampton Borough Council the power to determine bus services both within the Borough and those that crossed the border, along with routes, timetables, fare stages and fares themselves.

After the signing of the agreement, restriction on the picking-up and setting-down of passengers within Northampton Borough, previously mentioned within this book, were withdrawn. This allowed United Counties to use bus stops on the major roads served in and out of the town. The agreement gave Northampton Borough Council the right to operate around 83 per cent of the total mileage within the area, with United Counties being given 17 per cent of 52,630 miles per week. If mileage exceeded this, each operator was then entitled to operate 50 per cent of the excess mileage. Under the Northampton Agency Agreement, Northampton Transport held licences for the following services; 9 Bus Station–Moulton Park; 8 Kings Heath–Five Bells; 2/10 Kings Heath–Bushland Road; 11/14 Bus Station–Spinney Hill Road/Aintree Road; 12/13 Hazeldene Road–Dallington Green; 4/5 Bus Station–Headlands/Thirlmere Avenue; 23 Bus Station–Cliftonville Road/Delapre Park; 24/5/6 Holly Lodge Drive–Thorn Hill; a school service between Parklands Estate and the town centre and a second school service between Thorn Hill and Mereway School. United Counties held the licences for a number of services into Northampton, the majority of which were country area services. These were the 341/2/4 Bus Station–Daventry; 345 Bus Station–Daventry; 322 Bus Station–Bus Station; 323 Bus Station–Daventry; 292-5 Bus Station–Thrapston; 332 Bus Station–Horton Gates/Yardley Hastings; 129 Bus Station–Newport Pagnell/Turvey; 254/6 Bus Station–Corby; 595 Bus Station–Daventry/West Haddon;

316-9 Bus Station–Earls Barton/Old; 324-7 Bus Station–Market Harborough; 343 Bus Station–Great Brington; 363/5 Bus Station – Wellingborough; 339 Bus Station – Bus Station; 333/5/7 Bus Station – Buckingham; 128 Bus Station–Bedford; 338 Bus Station–Brackley; 330/1/530 Bus Station–MK–Bletchley; 346 Bus Station–Daventry.

In addition to these, a number of licences were held jointly by both operators. Of these, routes 1 Weston Favell Centre–Newton Road; 18/19 Acre Lane–Mereway; 3/7 Hopping Hill Estate–Rectory Farm and the 306 Bus Station–Weston Favell Centre were operated by Northampton Transport. Routes 305 Bus Station–Kings Heath; 307 Bus Station–Ecton Brook; 308 Southfields–British Timken; 304 Bus Station–Moulton Park; 300/1 Bus Station–Blackthorn; 309/10/1 Bus Station–Bus Station and the 363/5 Bus Station–Ecton Brook were operated by United Counties.

United Counties also introduced seven new services following the introduction of the agreement. These were as follows:

52 Bus Station–Old Duston–New Duston–Old Duston–Bus Station
53 Bus Station–Hardingstone–Wootton
54 Bus Station–Weston Favell–Ecton Brook–Blackthorn–Moulton Park
55 Southfields–Blackthorn–Ecton Brook–Weston Favell–Bus Station–British Timken
56 Bus Station–Weston Favell–Blackthorn
57 Bus Station–Weston Favell–Ecton Brook–Blackthorn
58 Bus Station–Weston Favell–Southfields

Following the results of the Market Analysis project conducted by the National Bus Company, United Counties routes in Northamptonshire underwent major revisions from 31 August 1980. A number of routes operating from Northampton were affected by these cuts.

The Northampton to Corby services were re-routed within Corby, operating via Oakley Road and Danesholme, taking new route numbers 253–256. Routes 292 to 295 (Northampton–Wellingborough–Rushden–Thrapston) were also replaced. A new route 293 commenced, operating between Northampton, Wellingborough and Rushden; whilst a new 294 ran between Northampton, Wellingborough, Rushden, Higham Ferrers, Raunds and Ringstead. Both of these new services incorporated the former Rushden town services.

Routes 330 and 331 (Northampton–Milton Keynes–Bletchley) had a significant frequency reduction from 31 August, with the link between Milton Keynes and Bletchley being withdrawn completely. The Towcester–Silverstone section of the 333 (Northampton–Gayton–Towcester–Silverstone) was also withdrawn from this date. Service 335 (Northampton–Blisworth–Towcester) was extended to serve Stony Stratford, Wolverton and Milton Keynes, replacing parts of the 330 and 331, along with the Greens Norton to Wolverton route previously operated by Basfords Coaches. The 336 and 337 (Northampton–Buckingham–Aylesbury) were also cut, the 336 being cut altogether from the Northampton area.

Routes 341-345, operating between Northampton and Daventry, were also altered from 31 August. From this date, the 341 continued to provide a link between Northampton, Weedon and Daventry, whilst the 345 linked Northampton with Nether Heyford, Weedon and Daventry, providing a half-hourly service between the two end termini. Daventry town service 350 was incorporated into these services. Routes 323 (Northampton–Whilton–Daventry) and 343 (Northampton–Whilton) were withdrawn at this time.

In amongst these service changes, 31 August saw the introduction of new route 340. This service ran between Northampton, Daventry, Coventry and Birmingham, operating on Saturdays and Sundays only. The limited-stop service 595 between Northampton, Long Buckby and Daventry was also retained. However, the 332 Northampton to Horton Gates service passed to Wesley's Coaches of Stoke Goldington.

Routes 316 to 319 were withdrawn from this date, affecting a number of villages close to Northampton, including Moulton and Overstone. Routes 253-6 were revised to cover the loss of these services in this area. The 363, 364 and 365 services between Northampton, Cogenhoe, Castle Ashby, Bozeat, Wollaston and Wellingborough were also withdrawn. A small link was still maintained on route 363 between Wollaston and Northampton.

The final cuts affected routes serving Harborough or Welford Road (324 to 327 and 246-248). These were replaced by two new services, the 324 (Northampton–Brixworth–Spratton) and 326 (Northampton–Spratton–Guilsborough–Welford–Market Harborough).

1981

Middleton Cheney-based Silverline Motors introduced three services in January 1981, running until December. Route 4 ran between Banbury, Middleton Cheney, Brackley and Northampton; route 5 operated between Banbury, Middleton Cheney, Marston, Greatworth, Farthinghoe, Brackley and Northampton. The final service, route 6, operated between Banbury, Middleton Cheney, King's Sutton, Charlton, Croughton and Northampton.

Palmerston Garage (Northampton) Ltd moved to the St James Mill Industrial Estate. In March, the company officially became known as Country Lion (Northampton) Ltd, the Country Lion name being used by the company for a number of years.

Mention has not been made of Richardson Coaches of Hartwell since 1961. In May 1981, the company started a seasonal service between Campbell Square, Northampton and Brighton and Eastbourne. This was started after a similar provision operated by National Express was withdrawn. Just prior to this, a Wednesday morning shoppers' service was introduced between Wicken Post Office and St John's Street, Northampton from 2 April. The service operated through Deanshanger, Old Stratford, Potterspury, Shutlanger, Stoke Bruerne, Ashton and Roade.

A handful of express services were introduced by Premier Travel of Cambridge in 1981. Two passed through Northampton. Route 70, jointly operated with Yelloway, ran from Rochdale and the Potteries and Cambridge/Ipswich, via Bedford and Northampton. A faster service to Blackpool ran via the M1 motorway.

Midland Red's route 596 was diverted to serve Yelvertoft from the 25 April 1981. Soon after, Midland Red was divided into a number of different operations, the 596 passing to the newly formed Midland Red South operation, based at Rugby.

A new service between Daventry and The Drapery commenced operation in November 1981, being operated by KW Services. This Monday to Friday service also served Weedon, Flore and Upper Heyford.

United Counties introduced a new coach service from 10 January. The 247 ran between Corby, Kettering, Wellingborough, Northampton, Coventry and Birmingham. From 26 April services 293 and 294 (Northampton–Wellingborough–Rushden–Ringstead) were altered, and a new service (295) was introduced to help distinguish between the routing through Rushden. At the same time the southern section of routes 324 and 326 were altered, the service to Gayton and Shutlanger being withdrawn and a limited service to these locations added to route 335. Route 337 was introduced at this time to operate on Wednesdays and Fridays between Buckingham and Northampton; whilst a daily service was introduced on the 340 (Northampton–Coventry–Birmingham). A new service between Northampton, Wellingborough and Burton Latimer was introduced on 4 November, using the newly opened A45 trunk road. The route was appropriately numbered X45.

1982

1982 opened with the sale of Richardson's Coaches of Hartwell to Buckinghamshire operator Souls of Olney, this taking place on 9 January, Souls took over the seasonal service to Brighton and Eastbourne introduced the previous year.

There was an introduction in November of a new service by Keyston Coaches. Running between Thrapston and Northampton, St John's Street via Woodford Green, Burton Latimer, Isham, Orlingbury, Little Harrowden, Mears Ashby and the Weston Favell Centre. It operated on Wednesdays only.

A new limited stop service was introduced from 27 March 1982. It linked Northampton and Heathrow Airport, running via Milton Keynes and Hemel Hempstead. Numbered 760, the route was placed under the Green Line brand and was operated by United Counties (two coaches) and London Country Bus Services Ltd (one coach). The end of March also saw revisions made to services 331 (Northampton–Milton Keynes) and 537 (Northampton–Towcester–Buckingham–Aylesbury).

United Counties introduced a Thursday only shoppers' service between Northampton, Wellingborough, Rushden and St Neots from 4 October 1982, this being numbered X93. A similar Wednesday only service between Moulton, Wellingborough and Bedford was numbered X94; whilst a Monday, Wednesday and Friday service between Northampton, Wellingborough, Thrapston and Peterborough was numbered X95.

1983

Jack Walker Minibuses of Merrifields, Bugbrooke commenced a service in January between Church Stowe Post Office and Northampton, Wood Hill via Upper Store, Nether Heyford, Upper Heyford, operating on the 1st, 3rd and 5th Wednesday of each month. No passengers were to be picked up between Nether Heyford, Canal Bridge and Northampton, Wood Hill.

A seasonal service was introduced between Southend, Colchester and Northampton from 1 May. The route was operated by Eastern National.

A new Northampton to London express service commenced operation from 18 September. The route terminated at Victoria Coach Station, and was operated by National Travel (East) Ltd. Another, more local, express service was introduced from 1 October. The route, operated by Yorks, ran between Weston Favell, Emmanuel Church and Luton Airport.

May 1983 saw the level of service offered between London and Northampton on the 249 and 250 services increased by United Counties. At the end of the month, a new service, the 696, was introduced between Northampton and Peterborough. However, the service was not successful and was withdrawn in September.

During 1983 the National Express network underwent a reorganisation. As a result, United Counties and Midland Red (East) Ltd took joint control of the service between Nottingham and Northampton from 18 September 1983. The Monday provision on the X95 (Northampton–Peterborough) was withdrawn from 5 October.

1984

Keystone Coaches introduced a second daily service into Northampton in January. The Northampton terminus was St John's Street, the service operated via Burton Latimer, Cranford, Woodford and Thrapston before terminating in Huntingdon. Certain journeys on the route diverted to Raunds. The service commenced operation from 30 June.

For a second year in a row, Eastern National operated a service between Southend, Milton Keynes and Greyfriars Bus Station, starting in February.

In April, the Grendon Community Minibus Committee took over responsibility for the minibus operation previously operated under United Counties. Various services connected the villages of Grendon, Easton Maudit, Castle Ashby and Whiston with both Northampton and Wellingborough.

National Travel (East) Ltd introduced a service between Bradford and Poole in June. The service operated via Nottingham, Leicester, Northampton, Luton in the eastern area before continuing south. It operated between 20 May and 19 November before being withdrawn. A second service was operated between 22 January and 21 July between Bradford and Bournemouth, serving Northampton amongst other locations on its journey.

A second community minibus scheme that had previously been under the control of United Counties became independent in September. The Gayton and Tiffield Community Minibus Committee operated routes between the two villages to either Northampton or Milton Keynes.

Midland Fox commenced operation of a service between Oadby and Northampton in November. It ran via Great Glen, Kibworth, Market Harborough, Maidwell and Brixworth.

United Counties altered a couple of services it operated under the Northampton Agency Agreement in April. The 56 and 57 (Bus Station–Weston Favell–Ecton Brook–Blackthorn) were withdrawn and replaced by an extension of the 1 and a new service numbered 51. The 1 ran between New Duston, Newton Road, Greyfriars bus station–Weston Favell–Thorplands–Goldings–Rectory Farm–Ecton Brook–Bellinge–Weston Favell–Bus Station. The 51 ran in an anti-clockwise direction over the same route, omitting Rectory Farm.

Northampton Transport's route 28 (Holly Lodge Drive–Bus Station–Camp Hill) was renumbered 8 in May. At the same time, a new Monday to Friday route was introduced numbered 17. It operated between Greyfriars–Horsemarket–Marefair–Black Lion Hill–West Bridge–St James Road–Weedon Road–Upton Way–Danes Camp Way–Ladybridge Drive–Shelfleys, returning to Greyfriars via Marefair, Gold Street, The Drapery, Sheep Street, Ladys Lane.

Jointly operated Green Line service 760 (Heathrow Airport–Northampton) was withdrawn from 29 September. Just prior to this the jointly operated X15 (Reading–Milton Keynes) service was extended northwards to Northampton to allow connections with the X61 to Leicester and Nottingham. The former service was operated by United Counties and Alder Valley.

By 1984 United Counties had a fleet of twenty-one coaches operating National Express contracts from a number of its garages, including Northampton. Two of these terminated in Northampton, these connecting the town with various towns, terminating in London and Bristol.

1985

London Country Bus Services commenced operation of two new services from Northampton to the coast. From 28 April services between Northampton and Eastbourne or Ramsgate began. Alongside these, a third service linking Rugby and Northampton with London.

In June, Northampton Transport introduced a new service between Greyfiars and Southfields/Standens Barn. The route served Horsemarket–Marefair–St James Road–Harlestone Road–Spencer Bridge Road, then either Gladstone Road, Mill Lane or St Andrew's Road, Kingsthorpe Road, Harborough Road, Holly Lodge Drive, Red House Road, Summer House Road, Deer Park Road, Brickyard Spinney Road, New Moulton Way, Lumbertubs Lane or Kettering Road, Lumbertubs Way, Billing Brook Road, Topwell Court, the return via Marefair, Gold Street, Drapery, Sheep Street to the Bus Station.

It has been mentioned numerous times throughout this book that Northampton Transport imposed a number of conditions on other operators to protect their revenue. Websters altered the route of their Grimscote to Northampton service in order to remove these conditions. The route was altered to operate via Banbury Lane, Danes Camp Way, Huntsbarrow Road, Rothersthorpe Road, Towcester Road, St Leonard's Road, Bridge Street, The Drapery and Sheep Street.

A number of routes within Northampton were altered in May 1985 when Abington Street was closed to traffic. 1985 saw the seaside specials operate for another year, the 601 running between Northampton and Mablethorpe. In June, a number of leisure services were introduced, centred on Northampton. The 693 ran to Stratford-upon-Avon on Sundays; the 694 to Windsor on Tuesdays and the 695 to Peterborough. The latter service operated on a Wednesday and replaced the X95. Northampton was linked with Banbury and the Cotswolds on Thursdays after the introduction of route 696. 697 ran between Northampton and Cambridge; the final service operating between Northampton and Lincoln, numbered 698. The Saunterbus was operated alongside these services. The 693 was withdrawn on 22 September, the 692 on 7 October. Route 695 was more successful, with a Friday service being added from 22 September. Another route to be withdrawn was the 537 (Aylesbury–Northampton), this taking affect from 30 August. At this time, the 335 (Northampton–Milton Keynes) also saw some alterations.

A second express service was introduced in November, using the A45 Nene Valley Way between Northampton and Wellingborough. The X94 ran between the two towns, continuing on to Raunds and Peterborough. A new service between Northampton and Roade, the 332, was introduced from this date. The 332 served a new housing development in East Hunsbury as well as the newly-opened Tesco store at Mereway. This date also saw the 335 cut to terminate at Paulespury. The 336 was a new service introduced between Northampton, Towcester and Milton Keynes, providing a more infrequent service than the 335. The Northampton–Birmingham route 340 also reverted to a Saturday only operation.

1986

A number of express coach services were introduced in May by both Premier Travel and United Counties. Premier Travel introduced route 40 from 17 May, a summer season service operating between Northampton and Cromer. The route called at St Neots, Cambridge, Ely, King's Lynn and Hunstanton on the way, ceasing operation from 20 September.

Hanslope based E&T Johnson commenced operation of a new service in May 1986 connecting Northampton with Stony Stratford. The route served Mereway, Wootton, Roade, Ashton, Grafton Regis, Yardley Gobion and Potterspury.

A month later, Cambus Limited began operating a route between Greyfriars and Corby Bus Station, running via Kettering, this being given route number A. Route B was a Sunday service operating between the two same locations. It operated via the A45, Great Harrowden and Kettering.

Geoff Amos commenced operation of a service between Daventry, Weedon, Flore, Upper Heyford, Nether Heyford, Kislingbury, Bugbrooke, Harpole and Northampton in May. The route operated Mondays to Fridays. The route was numbered N304.

E&T Johnson commenced operation of a second service into Northampton. This time it ran from Bletchley Bus Station via Central Milton Keynes, Hartwell, Ashton, Roade, Courteenhall, Quinton Green, Quinton, Wootton and Northampton. The route took number 33. In the same month, Midland Fox introduced a Wednesday and Friday only service between Clipston, Welford, Guilsborough, Creaton, Ravensthorpe, Spratton and Greyfriars.

Yorks reintroduced a service between Greyfriars and Cogenhoe numbered Y4. It was routed to serve Great Houghton, Little Houghton and Brafield, operating Monday to Friday.

Keystone Coaches operated a new service linking Thrapston and Northampton with the villages of Islip, Woodford, Cranford, Burton Latimer, Isham, Orlingbury, Little Harrowden and Mears Ashby. The route commenced operation in December, operating one journey on a Wednesday.

Grendon Community Minibus Committee commenced a route between Grendon, Easton Maudit, Castle Ashby, Whiston and Northampton in December. The route operated a single return journey on Wednesdays and Saturdays.

The closing months of 1986 saw Northampton Transport lose route 60 (Northampton–Boughton–Pitsford–Brixworth–Spratton–Creaton–Hollowell–Guilsborough). It was re-awarded to Country Lion, who operated three journeys a day Monday to Friday.

From 25 May United Counties introduced the Coachlinks brand, the intention being to connect at Bedford to allow transfers to other services, as well as providing connections with various National Express services. Two of the three new services ran to Northampton; these being the X2 (Northampton–Bedford–Luton–Luton

Airport) and X3 (Cambridge–St Neots–Bedford–Northampton). Alongside these routes, existing services X32 (Northampton–Milton Keynes–Buckingham–Oxford); X61 (Northampton–Market Harborough–Leicester–Loughborough–Nottingham); X64 (Kettering–Wellingborough–Northampton–Daventry–Coventry–Birmingham) and X94 (Peterborough–Raunds–Rushden–Wellingborough–Northampton) were added to the brand. There was a new service between Northampton, Old Duston and Harpole introduced in July, taking up route number 43.

The introduction of deregulation of the UK bus industry in 1986 meant that bus operators in the UK were required to register which services they wished to continue operating from October. A couple of local operators registered services in competition with United Counties, operating into Northampton. Yorks Brothers registered a service between Northampton and Daventry, via Nether Heyford and Weedon. At the same time, P&M Coaches of Northampton registered two town routes. The first was to operate between Northampton bus station and New Duston; whilst the second ran between Northampton and Wellingborough. However, these latter two applications were withdrawn by P&M Coaches.

From October, a number of service revisions took place, some of which affected services entering Northampton. Route 31 (Northampton–Wolverton) was extended to Central Milton Keynes. A second service, the 37, was introduced between Northampton, Stony Stratford and Milton Keynes. Route 38 (Northampton–Brackley) was extended south to Oxford. United Counties withdrew route 92 between Bozeat and Northampton, this being replaced by Yorks Travel. Leisure service 698 (Northampton–Lincoln) was renumbered 98. Peak hour journeys on Country Lion's service 60 (Northampton–Oxford) were added.

A couple of alterations were made to the Coachlinks network, with an increased service on the X32 being introduced, this making it slower than the newly introduced 38. The X61 also gained additional journeys on Sundays.

Thirty-five routes in Northamptonshire were placed for tender in July, with United Counties winning thirty of these, Northampton Transport being successful in winning the other five.

It may be recalled that, in 1979, Yorks took over the Northampton–Stoke Goldington–Milton Keynes service of Wesley's Coach Services. In 1986 the route finally gained a route number, the Y1. From 26 October, Yorks Bros. introduced a pair of services in direct competition with United Counties. The first was the Y2 (Northampton–Earls Barton–Wilby–Wellingborough–Finedon–Irthlingborough), competing with the 25, 46 and 47. The second ran the other way to Daventry, serving Kislingbury, Bugbrooke, Nether Heyford and Weedon competing with United Counties services 40 and 41. A fourth, less threatening service was introduced, the Y4. The route ran between Yorks' home village of Cogenhoe and Northampton. The Northampton to Milton Keynes route was also met with minor competition from Johnsons Coaches of Hanslope.

From 2 February, Milton Keynes Citybus commenced operation of route 331 between Northampton and Milton Keynes. The route also served Hardingstone, Wootton, Ashton and Hartwell on its journey between the two locations.

From the same date Luton & District commenced operation of a service between Northampton and Milton Keynes. It was jointly operated with United Counties, Thames Valley and Aldershot and District, as well as Milton Keynes Citybus.

1987

Websters Coaches withdrew their service between Grimscote and Northampton during 1987 as a result of low passenger numbers. However, the link between the two locations was not lost, Goode & Wootton took over the service with Northamptonshire County Council providing providing financial help. The route served Cold Higham, Fosters Booth, Pattishall, Ascote, Eastcote, Gayton, Rothersthorpe and Briar Hill.

Midland Red (South) Ltd withdrew its route 596 (Northampton–Rugby) from 27 July, the route being renumbered 96 from this date.

On 25 January United Counties' Friday only service 93 between Northampton and Bedford was withdrawn. During the early part of the year, the company entered a partnership with the Derngate and Royal Theatres in Northampton, along with Zetters Leisure and Social Club in Northampton. At this time, United Counties provided a service from these facilities to neighbouring towns.

Alterations were made to some country services operated by United Counties, taking affect from 8 March. The 31 (Northampton–Milton Keynes) was withdrawn and replaced by a new Coachlinks service numbered X34. This was done to further compete with Johnson's Coaches of Hanslope who operated over a similar route. The Northampton to Wootton section of this service was added to the Northampton to Brixworth service, which from this date, took up service numbers 31 and 31A. At this time, the 37 (Northampton–Milton Keynes) lost the section of route between Northampton and Towcester; whilst the 38 (Moulton–Oxford) was shortened to operate between Moulton and Paulerspury. A new Coachlinks service, the X38, was introduced between Northampton, Towcester, Brackley and Oxford. The Northampton to Kettering section of service 39 (Northampton–Kettering–Desborough) was withdrawn from 8 March.

United Counties introduced new route X46 linking Northampton with Wellingborough and Irthlingborough in March. The route was introduced to compete with York Bros. service Y2, as well as providing a more regular service by United Counties between Great Billing Turn and Northampton. A handful of services were withdrawn at the expense of this new service. Route 60 (Northampton–Guilsborough) was put up for re-tender, and was won by Northampton Transport. The 92 (Northampton–Bozeat) and 93 (Northampton–Wellingborough–Bedford) were also withdrawn. Route 96 between Yelvertoft and Northampton was also withdrawn, this being taken over by Midland Red South.

A month later, on 5 April, United Counties introduced a Sunday evening circular service between Northampton, East Haddon, Long Buckby, Weedon, Bugbrooke, Harpole and Harlestone; the service taking up route number 333.

Two new excursion style services were introduced from this time numbered 134 and 135. Operating from the Bedfordshire villages of Milton Ernest, Sharnbrook and Harrold, these travelled to either Northampton or Milton Keynes, commencing service on 2 May. From 10 May, the 31 series of routes gained another variation. The 31B commenced operation from this date, running between Northampton, East Hunsbury and Wootton.

Unlike previous years, the Saunterbus service around Northamptonshire did not run. However, United Counties operated a service linking Northampton with a number of local tourist attractions, to Holdenby House, Coton Manor Gardens, Guilsborough

Grange Wildlife Park and Grange Lodge Mini Farm Park. The route took up service number 31. Route 86 (Northampton–Wellingborough) was withdrawn from 26 July.

On 30 August there were minor timetable changes to services in the Northampton area. From this date, the route between Northampton, Towcester and Milton Keynes was reinstated after route 37 was extended northwards from Towcester. The route also served Roade and Yardley Gobion and replaced the Milton Keynes to Northampton part of the X32 which was withdrawn. The X38 (Northampton–Oxford) had its frequency cut from this date.

United Counties replaced the X46 (Northampton–Irthlingborough) in September with a new service numbered 45. At the same time, United Counties introduced a handful of school routes. The 824 ran between Little Billing and Moulton School; whilst the 839A/B/C operated between Wellingborough or Whiston and Northampton Roman Catholic Schools. 18 November saw the Wednesday and Friday link between Bozeat and Northampton reinstated.

From 22 November, Midland Fox introduced a new service, the 46B, linking Northampton, Wellingborough and Kettering, this being an evening service.

Northampton Transport introduced a new cross-Northampton service from 2 March. It operated between Kings Heath and Weston Favell Centre. It served St James, Greyfriars, Birchfield Road, and was numbered 15. A week later route 60 (Northampton–Guilsborough) was once again operated by Northampton Transport, taken over from Country Lion. The former company introduced three new routes between June and September. In June, route 16 commenced operation between Greyfriars, Towcester Road, Mereway, Tesco and Camp Hill. Route 95 (Greyfriars–Deer Park Road (Anglia Building Society) commenced operation on 5 July; whilst route 43 (Greyfriars–Duston–Harpole Church) began on 1 September.

1988

In February, the partnership of Goode and Wootton was dissolved. From this date, the two commenced separate operations. Goode Coaches of Boothville took control of the Grimscote to Northampton service, making some alterations to the timings. At the same time, R.I. Wootton started up a new company named Hunsbury Coach Travel.

On 3 October, Brittains Coaches Ltd commenced operation of a service between Flore, White Hart and The Drapery. It served The Heyfords, Bugbrooke, Kislingbury and Harpole on its journey in. Two journeys were provided between Flore and Northampton with one return journey. The route provided a workers' service for various shoe factories in Northampton.

United Counties introduced a new Sunday only route, the 222, from 14 February, linking Northampton and Brafield. Later in the year, a Tuesday only service was introduced between Northampton's Eastern Districts, Newport Pagnell, Milton Keynes and Buckingham, this taking up number 35. This service provided a link with route 197 to Woburn Abbey.

United Counties acquired York Bros. two stage carriage services between Northampton, Wellingborough and Irthlingborough and Northampton to Nether Heyford on 30 August. An agreement was made between the two operators that neither would establish stage carriage services in existing operating territories. At this time, Yorks were operating a service between Northampton, Hackleton, Newport Pagnell and Milton Keynes, along with a second between Northampton and Cogenhoe.

United Counties further revised services in the Northamptonshire area on 3 September and 13 November, including the withdrawal of Sunday route 46A (Northampton–Raunds), the journeys being incorporated into route 46 (Wellingborough–Raunds). From 13 November, Yorks routes Y2, Y3 and Y22 were de-registered. To compensate, some journeys on routes 45, 46 and 47 were diverted to serve the Weston Favell Centre. Timings on the 40 and 40A were also revised, incorporating journeys on the 38 (Northampton–Moulton) and 43 (Northampton–Harpole).

On 14 November, the majority of journeys on the 31B terminated at Butts Road, not continuing on the circular route around Wootton itself. Route 35 (Northampton, Eastern District–Buckingham) was also withdrawn from this date.

The final service revisions for 1988 meant that United Counties routes 45 to 47 lost their Sunday service. They were replaced by another service operated by Buckby's Coaches under contract to Northamptonshire County Council. Route 48 (Northampton–Bozeat) was also withdrawn from this time.

Northampton Transport introduced another new town service from 18 April. This was numbered 14 and ran between Greyfriars, Wellingborough Road, Park Avenue North and Parklands. The company was also awarded the Northamptonshire Saunter Bus contracts which started from 26 June. These ran from Greyfriars to various tourist attractions across the county. Route 17 (Greyfriars–Mereway) was withdrawn from 5 September.

1989

A new Wednesday only service was introduced by Jeffs Coaches of Helmdon from 24 May. It ran between Banbury and Northampton, via Brackley.

Coopers of Rothwell commenced operation of a new service, the 46B, introduced to operate between Northampton and Raunds, The Square. The Sunday and Bank Holiday service commenced operation on 18 September. A second, the 62B, was introduced from 1 October to operate between Rothwell High Street and Greyfriars Bus Station. This was a Sunday only service which provided one journey in each direction from 1 October.

Northampton Transport recycled route number 17 in January 1989 when they reused the number for a route connecting Greyfriars with Duston, Port Road/Quarry Road. The route also served St James Sainsburys, Gambrel Road, Ryeland Road and Weggs Farm Road. Northampton Transport introduced another local service linking Greyfriars with Northampton General Hospital in April. The route was numbered 29. Route 3B (Northampton–Althorp House) was cancelled by the company from 27 May. A new Saunterbus service between Northampton and Oundle Market Place was introduced between 28 May and 27 August. It linked the two locations with Rushden, Raunds, Thrapston and Lilford. A third new service was introduced from 4 September numbered 28. It ran between Greyfriars, Upton Sainsburys and Hopping Hill. A month later, circular service 800 was withdrawn.

1990–1999

1990

H.F. Cooper, trading as Buckby's Coaches, introduced a daily service between Northampton, Mears Ashby, Wellingborough and Raunds from 2 September.
A Wednesday only variation was also introduced, operating from Northampton to Desborough. Buckby's were already operating a Sunday and Bank Holiday service between Rothwell High Street and Northampton, this latter service starting in January.

On 2 June, Goode Coaches introduced a Saturday only service between Greyfriars and Cogenhoe, Royal Oak.

A Wednesday only service was introduced by Milton Keynes Citybus Ltd between Bozeat, Wollaston and Northampton from 7 November. One journey in each direction was provided on this route.

In March 1990 Coachlinks service X61 (Northampton–Leicester–Nottingham) on a Sunday and Bank Holiday Mondays was diverted to serve Foxton Village and Foxton Locks in Leicestershire.

A number of alterations were made to the Coachlinks network from 2 September 1990. On the X2 between Northampton, Bedford and Luton, a number of evening journeys were discontinued. The Cambridge terminus of the X3 (Northampton–Bedford–Cambridge) moved from the Rail Station to the Grafton Centre.

In September, United Counties regained the contract for the Sunday 46A service between Northampton and Raunds from Buckby's Coaches. Also at this time, the 45/46/47 group of services between Northampton and Wellingborough had diversions of the services to serve the newly opened Sainsbury's Superstore on Northampton Road, Wellingborough added.

From 2 December another change was made to the Northampton–Bedford–Cambridge X3 service. It was diverted in the Cambridgeshire village of Hardwick to serve the Limes Estate, providing an hourly facility to Cambridge from this village.

A handful of service changes were introduced by Northampton Transport. From 6 May, the 3A tourist service to Althorp House and Salcey Forest was withdrawn, being replaced by an extension of one of the Saunterbus services from Greyfriars to Stoke Bruerne, Blisworth and Milton Malsor. From 20 May, a new Saunterbus service was introduced from Northampton, serving Weedon, Daventry and Sulgrave Stores. Another new service, the 31B, was introduced from 8 September. The route provided one morning journey between Greyfriars and Wootton, Berry Lane.

1991

On 7 September, Buckby's Coaches introduced two new services into Northampton. The first, the 46B, operated between Wellingborough and Northampton via Wilby and Earls Barton. The second operated between Greyfriars, Brixworth, Lamport, Maidwell, Great Oxendon and Market Harborough. Both services were Saturday-only routes. On 4 September, a new service between Rothwell and Greyfriars commenced operation. It also served Clipston, Welford, Thornby, Spratton and Chapel Brampton. Numbered 59B, it operated on Wednesdays and Fridays during school holidays, and on Saturdays throughout the year. One return journey a day was provided on the route.

A number of United Counties services in the Northampton area were altered from 7 April 1991. Firstly, the 31B (Northampton–East Hunsbury) was revised in the southern area of the town and diverted to serve Forest Hill Road and operating a circular route around Butts Road. This service operated on an hourly frequency. On this date, additional journeys were added to the Coachlinks X38 service between Northampton and Oxford. The 38 (Northampton–Towcester–Whittlebury) saw, once again, a handful of journeys extended to Milton Keynes.

United Counties took on the operation of some services in the Northampton area on Sundays. Firstly, the 31 and 31B (Northampton–East Hunsbury/Wootton) gained a Sunday service. This was also the case for town service 16 (Bus Station–Shelfleys) which was operated by Northampton Transport Ltd on Mondays to Saturdays. The 59 between Market Harborough and Northampton was withdrawn from the Clipston area, discontinuing the Saturday Northampton to Clipston and Wednesday Market Harborough to Clipston services.

On 2 December a number of journeys on the 51 (Duston–Town Centre–Eastern District) were diverted to serve the Rectory Farm area of the town.

Northampton Transport introduced route 93 from 28 October. This Monday to Friday service linked Lodge Farm Industrial Estate with Brackmills Industrial Estate, running through St Giles Park, Duston, Kings Heath, St James and the town centre.

1992

On 1 September, a new service began, linking Milton Keynes and Northampton, operated by E&T Johnson of Hanslope. Numbered 72, the route also served Fosters Booth, Astcote Green, Pattishall and Rothersthorpe. This Monday to Friday route was short-lived, being withdrawn from 2 December.

From the same date, Milton Keynes Citybus introduced another service into Northampton. Numbered 38A, the route operated into the town from Towcester, Roade and Blisworth. Like the X24, the route operated Monday to Friday, operating one return journey.

On 19 October, Country Lion introduced a handful of local services within Northampton. Route 6 (Greyfriars–Dallington–Weston Favell–Greyfriars) and route 54 (Lower Farm Road, Moulton Park–Southfields–Blackthorn–Ecton Brook–Standens Barn–Weston Favell Centre) ran Mondays to Saturdays, whilst route 9 (Greyfriars–Moulton Park Industrial Estate–Round Spinney Industrial Estate–Round Spinney) operated Mondays to Fridays.

By 26 April, the Sunday town service network in Northampton was altered. The 31/31B were diverted to incorporate Hardingstone and Wootton into the service previously covered by the 16. These changes were originally intended to take place on the 5 April. It was from this date that a Sunday service was added to route 40 between Northampton Bus Station and Moulton Leys.

From 1 September 1992, further changes were made to Northampton area services 31 and 31B; the latter service was renumbered 30. After this date, the services ran a circular route serving East Hunsbury, Wootton and Hardingstone. Services 34, 37 and 38 which operated over various routes between Northampton and Milton Keynes were also altered along with the introduction of facilities to Milton Keynes Hospital.

18 October saw the introduction of a new express service operating solely in the Northampton area. The X25 operated between Northampton Bus Station and the unofficially named Northampton Coachway located at the Rothersthorpe service station on the M1. Operating seven journeys a day, this service was designed to coincide with crew changes on National Express services using the motorway. A week later, on the 26 October, an evening journey on Coachlinks service X2 between Bedford and Northampton had an extension added to the Beacon Bingo Hall in Northampton.

Northampton Transport commenced operation of the Christmas Park & Ride service from 21 November. The route operated from Cliftonville House Car Park to Mercers Row, via Bedford Road. It operated for the five Saturdays on the run up to the festive period.

1993

A new Wednesday only service was introduced from 19 March linking Scaldwell and Northampton. The route was operated by Hardingstone Taxis of Northampton.

Buckby's routes 46B and 62B, introduced in 1991, were both cancelled from 10 April. At the same time the Raunds service was also withdrawn.

On 17 April, amendments were made to Coachlinks service X65 Northampton–Kettering–Peterborough, with through journeys and short journeys being introduced between Kettering and Corby.

The extensions of routes 34/37/38 (Northampton to Milton Keynes) services had the provision to Milton Keynes Hospital withdrawn. From April a new school service was introduced between Northampton and Roade School, numbered 35. The X25 service that had been introduced in 1992 between Northampton Bus Station and the service station at Rothersthorpe on the M1 was withdrawn on 27 May 1993. The service was partially covered by the diversion of some journeys of route 38 to the facility.

A decision was made by Northampton Borough Council to sell its transport company, Northampton Transport Limited. United Counties took its chance and launched a competition with Northampton Transport, with the main aim of making it as unattractive to a potential buyer as possible. The first attack was the reduction of fares on services in similar areas that Northampton Transport was operating. The second part was the introduction of two new services which commenced on 31 July 1993. Route 80 provided a ten-minute frequency between Northampton Bus Station, Kingsthorpe and Chalcombe Avenue, the service travelling along Harborough Road, which was seen as one of Northampton Transport's more lucrative corridors. The second was the 85, which operated from the Bus Station to Thorn Hill and Danes

Camp, located in the south-west of the town. This Monday to Saturday service operated on a 20-minute frequency, and with low fares. In retaliation, Northampton Transport registered half-hourly services between Northampton, Moulton, East Hunsbury and Earls Barton, along with hourly services to Bellinge and Great Billing. However, these services did not have the effect on United Counties that Northampton Transport had hoped. From 4 October, these services were rerouted to serve Gold Street and The Drapery to make the shopping area more accessible. At the same time the 85 was routed to operate along Danes Camp Hill, Hunsbury Hill Road to Dayrell Road Roundabout. The Ringway, Thorn Hill and Ashbrow Road area of the route was discontinued.

The Northampton to Oxford X38 service no longer served the Cuttleslowe Park area in Oxford from 31 August.

Northampton Transport was sold by Northampton Borough Council to GRT Holdings of Aberdeen on 14 October 1993. Both the new owners and Stagecoach were quick to return to a non-competitive operation in the town. From 16 October 1993, Northampton Transport returned to their normal fare levels, with United Counties following suit in October. The main agreement centred around the provision of future services in Northampton. As has been mentioned, United Counties services 80 and 85 were operating over some of Northampton Transport's prime routes. A compromise was made between the two operators whereby United Counties would withdraw the 80 and 85 in return for four of six journeys on service 1 to the Eastern district of Northampton and the entire route 15 (Bus Station–Wellingborough Road–Bushland Road). The 80 and 85 were de-registered from 11 December 1993, with Northampton doing the same for its competitive services to Moulton, East Hunsbury, Great Billing and Earls Barton.

Four new services were introduced by Northampton Transport from 16 August. Another incarnation of the 17 was introduced, running between Greyfriars, Towcester Road, East Hunsbury and Butts Road, operating Mondays to Fridays. Route 12 linked Greyfriars with Kettering Road, Manning Road and Moulton, terminating at the Co-op. Route 29 was a circular service running from Greyfriars to Bellinge and Great Billing, running via Wellingborough Road. The final service was the 91 which operated between Greyfriars, Weston Favell, Great Billing, Ecton, Earls Barton and Dowthorpe Hill. Routes 12, 29 and 91 were all withdrawn from 13 December 1993, with route 15 being withdrawn two days before these. Route 16 (Greyfriars–Towcester Road, Cemetery Gates) was cancelled by the company on 23 August. As with the previous year, Northampton Transport again operated the Christmas park and ride service. This time, the car park was located at the Sixfields Stadium.

1994

Buckinghamshire Road Car Ltd commenced operation of a new service, the 32, between Bletchley, Milton Keynes and Northampton. The route ran via Castlethorpe, Hanslope, Hartwell, Ashton, Roade and Wootton. The route provided seven return journeys Monday to Saturday, commencing operation on 13 January.

From 6 January 1994, the evening journey to Beacon Bingo in Northampton on Coachlinks service X2 from Bedford was altered to operate on a Thursday night.

During 1994, York Bros. of Cogenhoe no longer thought it profitable to operate its service between Milton Keynes and Northampton that it had acquired from Wesley's of

Stoke Goldington in 1979. From 25 July 1994, United Counties took over the operation of this service, the 36, on hire until Yorks de-registered the service. However, this did not take place until 9 January 1995.

September 1994 saw the demise of service 38 between Northampton Bus Station and Rothersthorpe Services on the M1 was withdrawn.

On 3 October 1994 there was an addition of an X62 service between Northampton and Brixworth, enhancing the facilities offered on the regular 62 service. Most journeys on the X62 were diverted, under contract, to the Nene College Avenue and Park Campus sites.

Competition was met by both United Counties and Northampton Transport in November 1994. From 23 November, a new operator called Trinity Bus & Coach introduced a Monday to Saturday service between Greyfriars and Ecton Brook, via Wellingborough Road and Weston Favell Centre, numbered T1. The route competed with United Counties services 1 and 51. To compete, United Counties introduced new route 52 running from Abingdon Square to Standens Barn and Bellinge, via Wellingborough Road and Weston Favell Centre. Northampton Transport also introduced route 29 between Greyfriars and Ecton Brook to compete with the T1.

Northampton Transport commenced operation of route 100 (Northampton County Ground–Abingdon Avenue–Kettering Road–Town Centre–Rail Station–Sixfields Stadium). For a third year in a row, Northampton Transport operated the Christmas park and ride service. Again, it ran from Sixfields to The Drapery. Over the same period (November and December), the company operated route 80 between Greyfriars and Central Milton Keynes.

1995

The competition with Trinity Bus & Coach stepped up from 3 February when this independent revised its operations in Northampton and operated two services. The original T1 was replaced by two services, numbered T1 and T2 they operated from Northampton Bus Station to Weston Favell Centre, Ecton Brook, Rectory Farm and Blackthorn. The introduction of this operator to the Eastern District provided a faster link to the town centre than were currently being provided. The T1 and T2 operated a circular service from Northampton Town Centre serving Wellingborough Road, St Edmunds Street, Billing Road, St Giles Street and The Drapery then back to the Bus Station. This route also served Northampton General Hospital.

From 20 February 1995, United Counties withdrew its service 52 that they had introduced in 1994 to compete with Trinity. Instead, a new service numbered 50 was introduced to compete instead. The service operated from Northampton Bus Station to the Weston Favell Centre, then on to Blackthorn and Goldings before returning to the Weston Favell Centre and Bus Station. The 50 introduced a more direct service from Blackthorn to both the Weston Favell Centre and Northampton Town Centre. At the same time journeys on the 51 were diverted to serve Rectory Farm.

From 17 May 1995, the competition between United Counties and Trinity Bus & Coach in Northampton increased with the introduction of two new minibuses services, the 80 and 81. They ran on a circular service from the Weston Favell Centre via Blackthorn, Rectory Farm, Ecton Brook, Bellinge and Standens Barn, back to the Weston Favell Centre.

Northampton Transport altered service 29 to serve Weston Favell Centre and the full length of Ecton Brook Road. The 29 soon had its frequency reduced, and a new route, the 72, was also introduced. It operated in a similar fashion to United Counties services 80 and 81, running from the Weston Favell Centre, Rectory Farm and Ecton Brook before returning to the Weston Favell Centre.

Due to the large number of services operating in the Weston Favell area, there were not enough passengers to continue the profitable operation of services. This led to the withdrawal of the two services operated by Trinity Bus & Coach on 15 August 1995.

United Counties Northampton garage gained a somewhat unusual contract in June 1995. They supplied transport for rail workers from the Northampton area to the Stonebridge depot in North London.

On 25 September 1995 a new coach service was introduced to link Cambridge, Bedford, Milton Keynes and Oxford under the Stagecoach Express branding. Whilst this service operated outside of the study area of this book, two of the coaches used on the service were allocated to Northampton garage. To position the vehicles, a new early morning and late evening service commenced between Northampton and Milton Keynes numbered X6.

From the same date, new through services between Oxford, Northampton, Leicester and Nottingham were introduced as the X60 and X61 Coachlinks services. Links had been previously made between these locations on the X38 and X61, but the services were not separated. However, from this date the X38 was withdrawn. The X61 followed the route of the established X38 and X61 services. The X60 operated along the A50 between Northampton and Leicester, with some journeys diverted to Market Harborough. At this time, through workings on the X63 to Corby via Leicester and Nottingham ceased operation. The X62 service between Northampton, Nene College and Brixworth was also withdrawn from this date.

In April 1995, Grampian Regional Transport merged with the Badgerline Group to form First Group. Naturally, the Northampton operation became known as First Northampton.

1996

By 1996, Jeffs Coaches of Helmdon had acquired a Wednesday only contract to operate a service between Buckingham and Northampton. This was a market day shoppers' service.

On 8 January 1996 new through facilities were provided on the 38 and 40 Towcester services at peak times to serve the Northampton Grammar School located in nearby Pitsford.

The Buckinghamshire Road Car service 33 (Northampton–Milton Keynes) was transferred to the newly formed MK Metro Limited, who by 1996 were trading as Stagecoach Milton Keynes. The service operated Mondays to Saturdays, providing five return journeys.

A week later, Basford Coaches Ltd introduced a new workday service into Northampton. Route P1 commenced operation from 26 February, connecting Northampton with Blisworth and Roade.

A number of services operated by United Counties under tender in the Northampton area were altered from 15 April 1996. Firstly, service 50 (Bus Station–Blackthorn) and the competitive services 80 and 81 (Weston Favell–Blackthorn–Rectory Farm–Ecton

Brook–Bellinge–Weston Favell) were withdrawn and replaced by service 15 (Northampton Bus Station–Bushlands Road), this service being extended to the Eastern area of Northampton via the Weston Favell Centre, Goldings and Blackthorn.

There was an introduction of a new industrial service on 19 August, linking Northampton's Eastern district with the Riverside Retail Park and Brackmills Industrial Estate. The service took up number 53 and operated one journey in the morning peak, with a single return journey in the evening.

By September 1996, Northampton Transport had picked up a number of school contracts, operating outside of Northampton to other towns and villages in the county. This led to an increase in the number of second-hand vehicles into the fleet. A new service, the 84, linking Parklands and Brackmills, via Park Avenue was introduced on 30 September. The route provided two journeys a day Monday to Friday. Route B, the Christmas park and ride service, was again operated by Northampton Transport between Sixfields and The Drapery via St James.

1997

Further changes were made to United Counties Northampton network from 5 January 1997. The 15 (Bus Station–Weston Favell–Blackthorn) service was linked with routes 30 and 31 (Bus Station–Wootton–East Hunsbury) to form new services 15, 15A and 15B. The 15 operated to East Hunsbury and Blackthorn, whilst the 15A and 15B provided the service in the opposite direction, the letters denoting the direction they travelled in the southern part of the route. These services were introduced to serve the new Wootton Fields area of Northampton. In Blackthorn, the route travelled along Beaumont Drive and Thornfield rather than Wellingborough Road and Great Billing Way.

Further changes took place from 24 February 1997. Firstly, a new jointly operated service with Northampton Transport was introduced numbered 57. It provided a lunchtime link between Northampton Town Centre and the Brackmills Industrial Estate, operating on behalf of Barclaycard who had moved their operation from the Town Centre to Brackmills. A number of other services were introduced by other operators to the facility. At the same time, a new service, the 150, linked East and West Hunsbury with Brackmills operating similarly to the 53 mentioned under the 1996 heading. The 53 was increased from one to two journeys at this time, with the service stop serving the Riverside Retail Park.

From 3 March, Country Lion introduced nine local services. These operated Monday to Fridays to Brackmills. These routes were the 101 (Duston, Squirrels Public House, Main Road to Northampton, Pavillion Drive, Brackmills via Duston, St James and Far Cotton); 102 (Kingsthorpe, Boughton Green Road to Pavillion Drive, Brackmills via Kingsthorpe, Kingsthorpe Hollow and The Mounts); 103 (Kingsthorpe, Eastern Avenue North–Pavillion Drive, Brackmills via Kingsthorpe, Kinsley and Kettering Road); 104 (Moulton, Moulton Way–Pavillion Drive, Brackmills via Moulton Park); 105 (Thorplands, Billing Brook Road–Pavillion Drive, Brackmills via Thorplands, Goldings, Blackthorn, Rectory Farm, Ecton Brook, Bellinge and Standens Barn); 106 (Northampton, Towcester Road–Pavillion Drive, Brackmills via Briar Hill, West Hunsbury and East Hunsbury); 107 (Westbridge–Pavillion Drive, Brackmills via Marefair, Greyfriars and Abington Square) and 108 (Greyfriars– Bington Square–Brackmills–London Road–The Drapery–Greyfriars). Route 109 (Greyfriars to

Pavillion Drive via The Mounts and Abington Square) Saturday only service was also introduced at this time. A tenth service was introduced from 1 December numbered 110. This was a weekday lunchtime service that ran between St Giles Street, Derngate, Bedford Road to Pavilion Drive, Brackmills.

A handful of services were introduced by Northampton Transport over the course of 1997. The first two commenced operation from 8 April. Route 64 ran between Fosters Booth and Northampton, Monday to Friday. It served Ascote, Pattishall and Rothersthorpe. Route 57 was a local service, running from Freshfields to St Giles Street, running via Bedford Road. From 30 June, a circular route was introduced numbered 121. It ran from Greyfriars via St Andrews Road Monday to Friday. The Saturday operation was operated by United Counties. Later in the year, from 20 October, route 6 (Holmescross Road–Weston Favell Centre–Town Centre–Dallington Green) and 54 (Greyfriars–Ecton Brook–Blackthorn–Moulton Park) were introduced. Route 6 operated Monday to Saturday, whilst route 54 operated Monday to Friday.

1998

Geoff Amos commenced operation of a new Monday to Friday service between Northampton bus station, Old Duston and Harpole from 26 October. The route was numbered 43.

Country Lion introduced a trio of country services from 1 November, all of which operated on Sundays and Bank Holidays. The first was numbered 38C and operated a circular route from Sixfields to Roade, Stoke Bruerne, Shutlanger and Towcester. Sixfields was also the Northampton terminus of route 44C. The route also served Greyfriars, Riverside, Weston Favell, Moulton, Overstone, Sywell and Mears Ashby. The final route was the 61C, which provided a Sunday link between Northampton and Market Harborough. The route also served Chapel Brampton, Pitsford, Brixworth, Lamport, Kelmarsh and Arthingworth.

On 2 November, MK Metro Limited introduced route 37. The Monday to Friday service linked Northampton with Roade, Potterspury and Deanshanger. A week later, taxi operator D.L. Tear of Hardingstone introduced a Monday to Friday request service between The Drapery and the villages of Quinton, Courteenhall and Hartwell.

United Counties' Coachlinks services X60 and X61 (Nottingham–Leicester–Northampton–Oxford) jointly operated between Nottingham, Leicester and Northampton by Midland Fox cease. The latter operator withdrew from their part of the service. New journeys to Milton Keynes were added to the timetable for these services from 19 April. The Northampton to Raunds Coachlinks service X94 was declassified from 19 April 1998, numbered to the plain 94. Previous to this, the service had infrequently been operated by regular vehicles rather than Coachlinks vehicles.

Services to Irthlingborough Huxlow School and Raunds Manor School were both lost to Northampton Transport. However, in April 1998 this operator ceased its operation of these services. Therefore, United Counties diverted services 45/6/7 between Northampton and Irthlingborough or Higham Ferrers to serve these schools. 1/6/98

9 August 1998 saw a sponsored service introduced serving the new Swan Valley Industrial Estate. The route was numbered 42 and operated from Northampton Bus Station to the estate via Sixfields. Certain journeys on the 38 were also diverted into Swan Valley. From the same time, First Northampton discontinued the operation of its

route 8 (Town Centre–St David's) with the exception of a handful of journeys. United Counties took over the service with support from Northampton Borough Council. On 7 September the route was altered to operate from Harborough Road, Yelvertoft Road and Hastings Road instead of Cranford Road.

From 1 November 1998, United Counties introduced its first low-floor buses on the 15/15A/15B group of services. From this date, service 15 was dropped, the services operating as 15A and 15B. These new vehicles were branded as lo-liner.

A number of Northampton area services were also revised over the weekend of 1 and 2 November 1998. Route 36 Northampton to Milton Keynes underwent a significant revision, along with the 38 Northampton to Milton Keynes and the 39 Northampton to Kettering services. At the same time a new route was introduced numbered 44. This was a Monday to Friday service between Northampton and Mears Ashby.

United Counties applied for extra journeys on two rural services, with the finance coming from the Rural Bus Grant. From 1 November 1998, the company won route 59 (Guilsborough–Brixworth–Northampton), providing peak hour facilities Monday to Friday, along with the 66 (Northampton–Bugbrooke–Litchborough–Moreton Pinkney–Banbury). As well as these, additional journeys on routes between Deanshanger and Stony Stratford; Flore and Daventry; Northampton and Scaldwell, and Mears Ashby to Northampton were funded by the scheme.

Montague (Euro) Ltd was a new company which started operating in the Northampton area at the beginning of November 1998. Trading as A1 Buses, Montague commenced operation of a two-hourly service between Northampton and Daventry. The route was numbered A33 and also served Sixfields, Kingsbury, Bugbrooke, Nether Heyford, Flore, Weedon, Dodford, Southbrook and Dantere Hospital. From 5 January, the route was extended within Northampton to serve Northampton General Hospital. A second service, the A30, also started operating from the same date. The route connected the villages of Ravensthorpe, East Haddon, Church Brampton and Chapel Brampton with Northampton. A week later a third service was introduced, this time operating within Northampton itself. Numbered A34, this circular service ran from Northampton town centre to Kingsthorpe, Moulton Park, Moulton, Weston Favell and Ecton Brook before returning to the town centre. Commencing operation on the 11 November, it only lasted until 30 November when it was withdrawn. Neither United Counties nor Northampton Transport saw the need to react to this potential competition.

Northampton Transport withdrew route 84 from 20 April. From the same date, two new local services were introduced. Numbered 21 and 29, these routes linked Greyfriars, Northampton rail station and Acre Lane. On 1 July, the seasonal service 200 commenced operation, running from Greyfriars to Althorp House via Northampton rail station. Further service changes took place on 10 August. At this time Northampton Transport withdrew routes 2, 10, 17, 18, 19, 21, 24, 26, 29, 77 and 89. These were mostly replaced by several cross-town routes. New Monday to Friday service 17 was introduced at this time, operating between Brackmills and Kingsthorpe. It served London Road, Northampton town centre and Acre Lane. The other routes ran Monday to Saturday. New route 18 ran between Greyfriars, Gloucester Avenue, Mereway Tesco and Shelfleys. Routes 21 and 29 were reintroduced, along with the 30, operating between Acre Lane, Northampton town centre and rail station, terminating in Kings Heath. The final route was the 26 which linked Camp Hill and Obelisk Rise. It also served Far Cotton, the town centre, Eastern Avenue North and Holly Lodge

Drive. A new university service commenced operation from 28 September. It connected both the Park and Avenue Campuses with Greyfriars bus station. Naturally it only operated on weekdays during university term time.

1999

Midland Red South introduced a short-lived limited stop service between Milton Keynes rail station, Wolverton and Northampton rail station. The route started operation on 10 January and ceased on 21 March.

Yorks introduced a new park and ride service on 2 January, operating between Sixfields and The Drapery. However, York's involvement with the route was short-lived, the route passing to Geoff Amos from 13 March. The latter company introduced a new Monday to Friday service on 1 February. Numbered 95, it operated from Greyfriars to Moulton Park, running via North Western Avenue, Kings Park Road and Red House Road.

Yorks took over operation of Wednesday only route X24 (Bozeat–Wollaston–Northampton bus station) from 3 February. From 26 February, D.L. Tear (Hardingstone Taxis) commenced operation on a Friday and Saturday only request service between Horton, Piddington, Hackleton, Quinton, Wootton and Sixfields.

On 19 April, Head of Lutton started up route 204. This was a Wednesday only route that connected Thrapston, Burton Latimer, Orlingbury and Northampton.

Montague (Euro) Ltd introduced two new services to the Northampton area. The first started on 17 May numbered A36. It ran on schooldays between Nether Heyford, Bugbrook, Kislingbury, Harpole, Sixfields and Greyfriars. The second started on 23 November, numbered A38. It operated on Monday to Saturday between Greyfriars, Acre Lane and Nene College.

On 6 September, MK Metro started another service into Northampton. Route 43 linked Northampton with Roade, Stoke Bruerne and Towcester on Mondays, Tuesdays and Thursdays.

Geoff Amos was the last independent to start new services into Northampton in 1999. Starting on 1 November, the route ran between Northampton, New Duston and Long Buckby on Monday to Fridays. It was, however, a short-lived service, being withdrawn in December. The other service started on 17 November, running between Charwelton, Hellidon, Upper Catesby, Staverton, Badby, Newnham, Everdon and Northampton. It operated on the second and fourth Wednesday of the month.

United Counties made changes in January to routes in the Northampton area, most of these being minor. A more significant change was made to the 58 between Market Harborough and Rugby. The service was decimated and after this date it operated from Guilsborough, Welford, Husbands Bosworth and Market Harborough. Just two journeys operated in one direction, with one in the other on Mondays to Fridays. The 59 (Market Harborough–Welford–Guilsborough–Northampton) was also reduced, with the service between Guilsborough and Market Harborough being withdrawn from 4 January.

Route 94 (Raunds – Wellingborough – Northampton) was withdrawn from 5 September. The service was partially replaced by an extension of route 46 between Higham Ferrers and Raunds. In order to accommodate this extension, the Short Stocks area of Rushden lost its bus service. The 94 retained one single return journey from Northampton to Peterborough on a Saturday. Like other times when services were revised, the majority of the revisions were relatively minor. However, the 40 and 40A services (Nether Heyford–Northampton–Moulton) services were extended to Overstone and Sywell on an hourly basis, resulting in a reduction in the journeys on service 39 to these villages. On this latter service, two journeys were diverted via Brixworth and the A508 between Holcot and Northampton, these being numbered 39A.

Northampton Transport started 1999 by introducing a new Sunday and Bank Holiday service between Daventry, Upper Weedon, Flore, Nether Heyford and Northampton. Route 41F commenced operation on the 14 January. Route 46F commenced operation on 27 January. This Monday to Saturday service operated between Sixfields, Earls Barton, Wellingborough and Raunds. Two, more local, routes were introduced on 1 February. The 27 ran between Shelfleys, Mereway Tesco, town centre, rail station, Sixfields Retail Park and St Giles Park. Route 28 was the second new service and connected Links View Estate, St Georges Avenue, Northampton town centre and rail station, Sixfields Retail Park and Hopping Hill. Both routes operated Monday to Saturday. Another country service was introduced by Northampton Transport from 1 June. The route operated between Northampton and Crick via Church Brampton, East Haddon, Great Brington, Ravensthorpe, West Haddon and Yelvertoft. The final service to be introduced by Northampton Transport during 1999 was the seasonal service 200, operating between Northampton and Althorp House, this starting on 1 July.

2000–2009

2000

On 2 November 1999, competition arose in the Northampton area when Montague (Euro) Ltd, trading as A1 Buses, commenced a daily service between Northampton and Daventry on a two-hourly frequency. Two weeks later, a service was also registered in the Northampton area. Neither United Counties nor Northampton Transport felt the need to react to this competition. On 3 January 2000, the Eastern Traffic Commissioner revoked Montague's licence.

Jeffs Coaches introduced a new service on 22 January. The route was numbered 2 and linked Banbury and Northampton. The Wednesday only service also served Brackley, Silverstone, Towcester and Blisworth.

A new operator in the Northampton area was Nether Heyford-based J.M. Walker. Numbered DG222A, the route was another to link Daventry and Northampton. It also served Dodford, Weedon, Flore, Upper Heyford, Nether Heyford, Bugbrooke, Kislingbury and Harpole on Monday to Friday, starting on 4 September. Two days previous to this, D.L. Tear withdrew the Horton to Northampton service. Goode Coaches was another operator to withdraw its services from Northampton, doing so from 14 November.

Five new services were introduced by United Counties in the Northampton area during 2000. The first began on 4 January numbered 41A. It operated between Northampton, Nether Heyford, Weedon and Daventry. The others began on 30 May, all operating Monday to Saturday. Route 31 ran between Northampton, Blisworth and Collingtree before returning to Northampton. Route 42 was another service providing a link between Northampton, Flore, Weedon and Daventry. This started slightly earlier, on the 28 May. Route X5D was a short-lived limited stop service between Buckingham, Milton Keynes and Northampton. It was withdrawn by the end of October. The final service was the 16 which operated between Greyfriars, Wootton, Grange Park and Roade.

Northampton Transport introduced a new Monday to Friday service from 5 January numbered 411. It linked Ravensthorpe and Northampton, via East Haddon and Church Brampton. From 30 April the company withdrew route 41F that had been introduced the previous year.

2001

2001 proved to be a reasonably quiet year for bus service development in Northampton. The Sixfields to The Drapery park & ride service introduced in 1999 was withdrawn by Geoff Amos from 31 March 2001.

Two new routes were introduced by Country Lion over the course of the year. The first started on 23 April. Numbered 444, the route ran between Northampton, Weston Favell, Overstone, Sywell, Mears Ashby, Wilby and Wellingborough. It operated on Monday to Friday. The second was introduced from 5 November. It was numbered 111 and was a more local service, running from Duston to Northampton town centre, via Lodge Farm Industrial Estate and Harlestone Road, again being a Monday to Friday service.

April was a busy month for Northampton Transport, who introduced a number of new services following the withdrawal of routes 3, 3C, 7, 11, 14, 20, 26, 46F and the 69/79, these all ceasing to operate from 22 April. The following day, the following services were introduced:

2 Northampton–Kettering Road–Goldings–Blackthorn
3 Northampton–Kettering Road–Lake View Estate–Weston Favell Centre
3A Northampton–Kettering Road–Parklands
5/5A Northampton–Riverside–Weston Favell–Southfields–Ecton Brook
10 Rail Station–Bus Station–Northampton General Hospital–Brackmills
24 Northampton–Camp Hill via St Leonards Road and Briar Hill
26 Northampton–Obelisk Rise via Kingsthorpe
88 Kings Heath–St James–Parklands–Kettering
93 Northampton–Billing Road–Parklands

The following week, 28 April, saw the introduction of two new country services. These were the 107 (Northampton–Byfield–Banbury) and 475 (Northampton–Harpole). The final service alterations concerning Northampton Transport in 2001 were the withdrawal of the 22 from 1 September and the 26 and 54 from 26 October.

2002

Country Lion introduced two variants of route 9 on 8 April. The first ran from Round Spinney to Northampton town centre. It served Spinney Road, Holly Lodge Drive, Harborough Road, St Andrew's Road and St James Road. The second variant ran from Moulton Park to Greyfriars, also serving Holly Lodge Drive, Harborough Road, St Andrews Road and St James. Like other Country Lion services, the route operated Monday to Friday.

A week later Geoff Amos began a Saturday only service between Byfield and Northampton, running via Woodford House, Preston Capes, Blakesley, Maidford, Farthingstone and Litchborough. The service commenced operation on 15 April.

A couple of days later, on 18 April, SMS Executive Travel of Towcester started a Wednesday only service numbered BW222. The route operated between Byfield, Woodford Halse, Maidford, Bugbrooke, Kislingbury and Northampton. From 22 April a second service, this time only operating on Saturdays, was introduced by SMS. Taking route number RT206B, the route ran from Helmdon to Northampton, serving the villages of Weston, Towcester and Blisworth. The BW222 was short-lived, being withdrawn from 31 August.

Birmingham-based Bowens Group acquired the business of Yorks Travel in August. At the time of the takeover, Yorks were operating routes X24 and Y4 into Northampton, both taking different routes to Wollaston. The Yorks name was retained by Bowens.

United Counties introduced a new local service on 8 April. Numbered 9, the route operated a circular service from Greyfriars to Moulton Park and Kingsthorpe.

The Northampton to Roade service 16 was withdrawn by the company from 27 October.

In 2002 there was yet another reshuffle of Northampton Transport services. From 23 March, routes 8, 60 and 94 were withdrawn. A couple of weeks later, from 8 April, the existing local network of routes were re-organised. From that date, route 3 ran between Rectory Farm, Weston Favell, Northampton town centre and Rye Hill. 3A (Bus Station–Kettering Road–Moulton Leys) was introduced to operate on Sundays and bank holidays. 4/4a was a new cross-town service running between Obelisk Rise, Kingsthorpe, Northampton town centre and Headlands. Routes 5/5A served Camp Hill, Briar Hill, town centre and the Weston Favell Centre before travelling on to either Southfields or Ecton Brook. Route 13 provided a link between Greyfriars, St Georges Avenue and Links View Estate. Southfields and Moulton Park were connected to Greyfriars on route 54. Not to be outdone by United Counties or Country Lion, Northampton Transport also operated a route 9. Their variant ran between Greyfriars, Moulton Park and Round Spinney. The final new service to be introduced at this time was the 60, operating between Northampton, Spratton, Guilsborough and Welford.

On 24 June, Northampton Transport commenced operation on route 50 (Greyfriars–Mereway Tesco–Shelfleys), operating Monday to Saturday. The second new route to be introduced by Northampton Transport in 2002 started on 23 September. This was a Monday to Friday service linking the rail and bus stations with the University of Northampton, taking up route number 25. Two weekend night services commenced operation on 1 November. N1 ran a circular route from The Drapery to Far Cotton, Duston and Kingsthorpe. N2 operated in a similar fashion, serving Wellingborough Road, Bellinge and Rectory Farm. Both operated until 21 December, at which time they were withdrawn.

2003

Derek Stuart Taylor introduced two local services from 6 January. Numbered 8 and 8a, they operated from Fulford Drive and Greyfriars bus station, operating via Kingsley Road, Abington Avenue, County Cricket Ground, Park Avenue South and Billing Road.

Geoff Amos introduced a new Wednesday only service from 30 April to link Ravensthorpe and Northampton. The service was numbered GA08 and called at Great Brington, Little Brington and Harlestone on its journey to the town. This was a short-lived service, being withdrawn in October of the same year. 28 August also saw the withdrawal of route GA09 (Byfield High Street–Northampton, The Drapery).

Great Addington based Carters Travel commenced operation of a service between Weedon Lois, Helmdon and Northampton on the 1 May. The service operated as a hail and ride service, operating daily.

LQT Ltd of Watford began operating a new service between Milton Keynes, Newport Pagnell, Olney and Northampton from 6 October. The service was number 1 and operated Mondays to Saturdays.

Country Lion withdrew services 101 (Duston–Northampton) and 104 (Moulton–Northampton) from 19 December 2003.

MK Metro Limited began operating into Northampton from 28 April 2003 when they started service 36 between Milton Keynes and Northampton. The route operated Mondays to Saturdays and called at Newport Pagnell and Olney. A second service was started by MK Metro in November, this time being a Northampton local service. The 11 ran on a circular route from Greyfriars bus station to Kingsley Park, Parkland

and Moulton before returning. The 36 was withdrawn in mid-April 2005; whilst the 11 continued operating until the end of October 2010.

Three new local services were introduced by Derek Stuart Taylor of Potterspury, who traded as Meridian Bus, from 28 April 2003. Route 11 ran between Northampton town centre and Parklands, travelling along both Kettering Road and Wellingborough Road. The second, the 12, ran from the town centre and St George's Avenue to the University of Northampton. The third, the 14, operated between Weston Favell and the University of Northampton's Park Campus. It served Southfield, Thorplands and Round Spinney on its journey between the two locations. These were, however, short-lived and were withdrawn at the end of October 2003.

Yorks introduced a new service connecting the Weston Favell Centre and University with the various housing estates in the Eastern District and Moulton Park. This service was introduced in November, being withdrawn in mid-April 2004.

Northampton Transport withdrew route 13 (Greyfriars–Links View Estate) from 6 January, followed by routes 11 and 14 (Town Centre–Moulton) from the same date. Route 200 (Althorp House–Northampton) was withdrawn by Northampton Transport from 17 February. Service 411 between Northampton and Ravensthorpe on 24 April. A number of services were altered by the company on 18 July. The route between Thorplands and Northampton town centre took up new number 1C. Other service changes at this time affected various school services operated by the company. Route number 88 was allocated to the service running between King's Heath and Parklands. On 30 June a new circular service was introduced, operating via Bedford Road, this taking route number 63. Just before this, the routes serving the King's Heath and Acre Lane areas took numbers 21, 29 and 30. Northampton Transport introduced a new town service between Greyfriars and Ecton Brook on 28 July. Numbered 15, it operated via Wellingborough Road, Weston Favell Centre and Bellinge, operating on Monday to Saturday evenings. A number of school services were cancelled from 29 August, these being the 94 (East Hunsbury–Northampton School for Boys); 301 Cogenhoe – Northampton); 300 (Ecton Brook–Northampton) and 303 (Wellingborough– Northampton). Another route to be cancelled by Northampton Transport was the 17 (Kingsthorpe–Brackmills), this taking effect from 24 November. A new service, the 22, was introduced between Sixfields Retail Park and Duston, commencing operation from 1 December. This remained in operation until 9 April 2004, at which time it was cancelled.

United Counties withdrew a number of services that operated from Northampton to local attractions from 25 May. They were the 373A which ran to Daventry Country Park; 372 to Castle Ashby Farm Shop; 371B to Naseby Farm Museum and the 371A/374A/375A between Northampton and Corby. A Sunday only service, 36, was introduced on 3 May. This operated between Horton Gates, Piddington and Greyfriars.

Several new services were introduced from 28 July, along with some other alterations to Northampton services. The first was route 1 which ran between Duston, Greyfriars and Great Billing Turn. Routes 15 and 16 were introduced to run between Ecton Brook and Hardingstone, Wootton and East Hunsbury before returning to Ecton Brook via the town centre. The circular service between Greyfriars and Quarry Road, Duston was numbered 51 from this date. Route number 56 was allocated to a route that ran between Greyfriars and Swan Valley; whilst services operating between Beaumont Drive and Butts Road were numbered 15/15A and 15B.

United Counties also introduced three new local services in August. From the 7th of the month circular service 5c commenced operation, operating between Greyfriars, Camp Hill, East Hunsbury and Wootton. A second service was the 11, which ran between Greyfriars and Parklands. The latter route only lasted until 30 November; at which time it was cancelled. The following day route 3 commenced operation, running between Greyfriars, St James and Rye Hill.

2004

Nether Heyford based Go-Jak Buses withdrew both of its services to Northampton from the 27 April. These routes were the 222A (Daventry–Northampton) and 568 (Norton–Northampton).

April 2004 saw the introduction of two services by Carters Travel of Great Addington. The first was numbered W114 and ran between Grendon Post Office, Grendon, Easton Maudit, Bozeat, Wollaston and Northampton on a Wednesday. The second, numbered BW485, operated between Weedon Lois and Northampton. It also served Eydon, Banbury, Maidford and Litchborough. The W114 operated for a couple of years before being withdrawn on 10 October 2006.

Milton Keynes-based Sapwell Travel introduced a new service, the 36A, in the same month. This Monday to Saturday service ran between Little Linford, Stoke Goldington, Wootton Fields and Northampton.

Jeffs Coaches of Helmdon introduced a new Wednesday only service on 21 April. Route 3 linked Helmdon, Wappenham, Blakesley, Maidford and Litchborough with Northampton. The route continued to operate until the beginning of November.

A pair of limited stop services were introduced by SMS Executive Travel of Towcester on 19 April. First was the 222A which ran between Weedon and The Drapery, serving the villages of Flore, Upper Heyford, Nether Heyford, Bugbrooke, Kislingbury and Harpole. The service operated Mondays to Fridays. The second, numbered the 568, operated from the White Horse Pub in Norton to Greyfriars bus station. On its journey between the two locations, it served the villages of Whilton, Great Brington, Little Brington and Upper Harlestone, this only operating on Wednesdays and Saturdays. The 222A only lasted until April 2005 whilst the 568 was more successful, operating until the beginning of November 2010.

York Brothers withdrew their route X24 (Bozeat–Northampton) in April 2004. Later in the year, in November, Yorks commenced operation of the seasonal park and ride service from Cliftonville House to the town centre. The company also commenced operation of route Y4 between Northampton and Wollaston. The service ran via Great Houghton, Little Houghton, Brafield on the Green, Cogenhoe and Grendon. This was a new Monday to Friday service which started on 21 December. The Weston Favell Centre to University of Northampton service was numbered 54 at this point. The service remained operating until the beginning of September 2011.

2004 saw the introduction of the *Overground* network on Northampton Transport's routes. The *Overground* name was a brand used by First Group in the majority of its operations around the country.

The company introduced a new service, the 52, from 1 November. The service operated between Greyfriars, Wellingborough Road, Weston Favell Centre and Rectory Farm.

2004 saw three services withdrawn by United Counties. Routes 32 (Deanshanger–Northampton) and 36 (Horton Gates–Northampton) from 18 April. Route 21 (Duston–Bellinge) was withdrawn on 4 July. However, on the 18 April the X4 (Peterborough–Northampton) was extended from Northampton to Milton Keynes, being branded as Cross County at this time. It was operated by the first low-floor double-deckers in the United Counties fleet.

2005

Country Lion withdrew route 9 between Moulton Park, Round Spinney and Northampton bus station in March. The 444 (Northampton–Wellingborough) was next to be withdrawn, this being done at the beginning of June. Country Lion operated the Christmas park and ride service, commencing operation on 5 November. Numbered 622, the service ran between Cliftonville House and St Giles Street.

Goode Coaches withdrew two of its services to Northampton during April 2005. It was at this time that this operator's services between Grimscote and Northampton and Cogenhoe and Northampton ceased.

Corby-based independent Judges Minicoaches commenced operation of route 60 at the beginning of July. The route operated between Market Harborough, Cold Ashby, Guilsborough, Kingsthorpe and Northampton.

MK Metro significantly increased their presence in Northampton during 2005 with the introduction of a number of services. The first two commenced operation on 17 April numbered 86 and 87. These provided a link between Northampton and Towcester, continuing operation until September 2011. The next set of services were introduced in early September. The 43 and 43A provided a limited stop service between Northampton, Rye Hill and Harpole. However, these were both short-lived and were withdrawn in January 2006. September also saw the introduction of another local service. The 21 operating between St James, University of Northampton Park Campus and Moulton Park. The final service to be introduced by MK Metro during 2005 was the 22N. Operating between the town centre, Upton and St Giles' Park, this service started from 4 December. The latter service lasted just under three years, being withdrawn in November 2008. Route 21 was withdrawn in September 2010. The expansion of the Company into Northampton led to the opening of a new operating centre in the area. This was located at the premises of W. Wright and Sons, located in Old Station Road, Cogenhoe.

Several new services were introduced by Northampton Transport from 20 February 2005. The first ran between Greyfriars, Briars Hill, Towcester Road and Camp Hill, this taking route number 12. Route 7 was introduced to run between Greyfriars, Kettering Road, Booth Lane North and Churchill Avenue. This was followed by route 8 (Greyfriars–Kettering Road–The Headlands–Weston Favell Centre) and route 10 (Greyfriars–Kingsthorpe Road–Acre Lane). All four services operated Monday to Saturday.

Two additional new services commenced operation on 4 April. Route 28 ran between Greyfriars, London Road, Gloucester Avenue and Mereway Tesco; whilst route 1 operated between Greyfriars, Northampton railway station, St James Square and Newton Road, Duston. However, the day before these new services commenced operation, routes 15 (Greyfriars–Ecton Brook), 9 (Greyfriars–Round Spiney), 54 (Greyfriars–Moulton Park), 3 (Rectory Farm–Rye Hill) and 3A (Greyfriars–Moulton Leys) were all withdrawn.

Route 50 was introduced to operate between Weston Favell, Goldings, Rectory Farm or Blackthorn from 25 July, this operating until 7 November. From 23 July two services were withdrawn. These being the 1 (Greyfriars–Newton Road, Duston): 52 (Northampton–Rectory Farm). From 7 November, route 7 (Greyfriars–Churchill Avenue) was also withdrawn.

To counteract the introduction of the new services introduced in February by Northampton Transport, mentioned above, United Counties introduced new route K9. This was a circular service running between Greyfriars and Kings Heath. This started on 7 March. In April, several services were withdrawn by the company. On the 1 April, route 57 (Pavilion Driver–St Giles) ceased operation. It was followed on the 17 April by routes 31 and 87. A new Monday to Saturday service was introduced from 6 June. Numbered 38 the route operated between Northampton, Moulton, Mears Ashby and Wellingborough rail station. Further withdrawals took place in September, at which time routes 3 (Greyfriars–Rye Hill) and 9 were both withdrawn. A new town service was introduced from 7 November, operating Monday to Saturday. The route was a circular service operating from Greyfriars to the Lakes Estate.

2006

Country Lion introduced two new services in January 2006, both of which served the Beacon Bingo club on Weedon Road, Northampton. The first linked the club with St James Road, Marefair Horse Market, Lady's Lane and Greyfriars bus station. The second ran further afield, starting at Bletchley Bus Station, and served Waddon Way, Grafton Street, Milton Keynes Rail Station and Grafton Regis. Both services continued to operate until August 2008 when they were both withdrawn.

3 April 2006 saw the withdrawal of Buckby's Coaches' service between Desborough and Northampton. At the start of May Jeffs Coaches withdrew the service 69 between Buckingham and Northampton.

United Counties introduced several new services in the Northampton area during 2006. The first was numbered 404 and operated from Greyfriars to Rushden, Avenue Road via Wellingborough. Commencing on 30 April, two journeys a day were provided over the route, this being increased to eight from 1 May. From 23 July, revisions were made to routes 15 and 16, with the original services being cancelled from this date. The new route 15 ran from Greyfriars to Grange Park, located close to junction 15 of the M1 motorway. It also served Hardingstone and Wootton on its way. Route 16 linked Greyfriars Bus Station with Birchfield Road, the Weston Favell Centre, Bellinge and Ecton Brook. A third route, the 14, was also introduced from this date. It provided a circular service between Greyfriars and East Hunsbury. On 23 July, United Counties withdrew from the Northampton to Milton Keynes services 33 and 34.

2007

The final service introduced by MK Metro commenced operation in October 2007. Route 50 was won from Northampton Transport and continued to operate between Northampton town centre and Pineham. The 50 was operated by MK Metro until September 2010 when it was withdrawn.

Meridian Bus of Potterspury commenced operation of another local service in October 2007. Route 3 ran between Greyfriars Bus Station and Southfields. Like the local routes introduced by the company in 2003, route 3 was another short-lived service, being withdrawn at the beginning of March 2008.

On 21 January, United Counties withdrew routes X42 (Northampton–Daventry) and 40/41 (Northampton–Daventry, New Street). From this date the services between the two towns were re-launched as Daventry Dart and gained route numbers D1 and D2. The following day, another new service was introduced numbered 52. It operated between Greyfriars and the Brackmills Industrial Estate. The route operated Monday to Friday, providing three journeys a day. It travelled between the two destinations using Cliftonville Road and Bedford Road. This was the 204 and provided one journey in each direction between Thrapston, Woodford and Northampton on Wednesdays. A new limited stop service between Northampton, Market Harborough and Leicester was introduced from 2 September. The route was numbered X7, replacing the previous incarnation of the route. The final new service to be introduced by United Counties during 2007 started on 24 September. The route was numbered 20 and connected the University of Northampton's Park Campus with Abington Square and Wellingborough Road before returning to Park Campus. The service only operated during term time on Monday to Friday.

2008

In January 2008 several Country Lion services in Northampton were withdrawn. These were the 102 (Kingsthorpe–Northampton), 107 (Westbridge–Northampton) and 111 (Duston–Northampton).

Two Saturday-only services were introduced by SMS Executive Travel of Towcester in September 2008. They took up service numbers 250 and 251, and operated between Weedon Lois, Culworth, Eydon, Maidford and Northampton.

Souls Coaches of Olney, Buckinghamshire took on the contract for route 18 between Weston Favell Centre, Boothville, Moulton and the University of Northampton's Park Campus from 15 September. The service operated Mondays to Fridays.

The Northampton to Rugby services operated by Northampton Transport (205-208 group) were withdrawn from 3 August 2008. From the same date, route 57 (Town Centre–Brackmills) was also withdrawn. Later in the year, from the end of November, a new route 22 was introduced operating between Greyfriars, Sixfields, Upton, St Crispin, St Giles Park, Weggs Farm Road. This was followed by the withdrawal of route 27 (Shelfleys–St Giles Park) from 1 December.

United Counties started off 2008 by canceling routes 15C and C1 (Cliftonville House–St Giles). Two new services were introduced by the company from 4 May. These were numbered 9 and 9A and operated between Northampton and Duston. Two months later, on 27 July, United Counties withdrew from route 59 between Northampton and Welford. Route 17 (Greyfriars–Billing Aquadrome) was introduced by United Counties, operating on a two-hourly frequency.

2009

2009 was a quiet year for bus service developments in the Northampton area. Northampton Transport withdrew route 8 (Greyfriars–Weston Favell Centre) from 5 January. At the beginning of November, there was an introduction of a limited stop service between Norton, Whilton, Upper Harleston and The Drapery. Route G1 was introduced by SMS Executive Travel, operating on Wednesdays and Saturdays. The service continued operation until the beginning of September 2011 when it was withdrawn.

Withdrawals were also made by United Counties. Routes 29 and 30 between Greyfriars and Kings Heath finished on 3 January, followed by the 14A (Greyfriars–Grange Park) on 7 March. On 26 October the X88 between Northampton and Oxford was withdrawn. From the same date the company introduced new service 36, connecting Northampton with Olney.

2010–2019

2010

Centrebus took over the operations of Judges Minicoaches of Corby in August 2010. On 2 August there was an introduction of a new route, 60, between Market Harborough, Welford and Northampton, operating Mondays to Saturdays.

The new university term in September 2010 saw Country Lion win three services from Souls Coaches of Olney. These were routes 18 (Weston Favell Centre–University of Northampton, Park Campus); 19 linking the University of Northampton campuses; and route 10 (Sixfields–Park Campus). The 10 and 18 ran Monday to Friday, whilst the 19 was a Sunday only service, this latter service being withdrawn in December 2015. A month later, a fourth local service in Northampton was introduced by Country Lion. Numbered 11, the service ran between Spinney Hill Road, Kettering Road, Links View, Kingsley, Kingsley Park and Greyfriars Bus Station. The service continued to operate for a number of years, being withdrawn in December 2017.

Meridian Bus of Potterspury introduced two new services during mid-September. Route 86 ran between Greyfriars Bus Station, Greens Norton, Towcester and Roade before returning to Northampton. The second, the 87, operated between Greyfriars bus station and the Brave Old Oak in Towcester. Both were withdrawn from 20 March 2011.

In September 2010, Souls Coaches of Olney commenced operation of three services in Northampton, centred on the University of Northampton's Park Campus. Two routes commenced operation on 13 September. The first was the 19A and operated between Park Campus, Kingsthorpe, University of Northampton's Avenue Campus and Greyfriars bus station. The second was the 20 which ran a circular service from Park Campus, serving Kingsthorpe, Abington and Northampton General Hospital. The third service was the 21 which operated from the University of Northampton's Student Centre to Greyfriars bus station, operating via St Georges Avenue and Northampton General Hospital. This started a week later on 20 September. The routes were lost in September 2012.

First Northampton's route 22 (Greyfriars–St Giles Park, Weggs Farm Road) was withdrawn from 19 September 2010. From the same date routes 5/5A (Camphill–town centre–Southfields) were also withdrawn.

United Counties took up the slack on route 5 following the withdrawal by First Northampton. From 20 September, the new route 5 commenced operation between Southfields, Northampton town centre and Duston. From this date, United Counties also took up operation of circular service 22 (Greyfriars–St Giles). On 10 September there was the introduction of new routes 3 (Greyfriars–Rye Hill) and workers' service 50 (Greyfriars–Pineham). Just over a month later, on 25 October, a third new service, the 11, was introduced. It linked Greyfriars and Kingsley.

2011

Country Lion withdrew two services during 2011. The first, the 110 (St Giles–Brackmills), was withdrawn in April. This was followed in September by the withdrawal of university route 10 (Sixfields–Park Campus).

Yet another short-lived service was introduced by Meridian Bus of Potterspury in April 2011. This time the route ran between Northampton bus station and Mereway Tesco. Numbered the 42, it remained operational until the beginning of December.

Aylesbury-based Z & S International took over operation of route 33 and 33A between Northampton, Roade, Hanslope and Milton Keynes. The service commenced operation from 23 May.

United Counties withdrew two local services from 8 May. These were the 11 (Northampton–Kingsley) and route 12A. 21 March saw a new route, the 86, commence operation between Northampton and Rothersthorpe, with a two-hourly extension to Greens Norton and Towcester. From 4 September, the latter extension became a permanent fixture of the route. From this date, a second service was introduced between Northampton and Towcester, numbered 87. It was joined at this time by route 88, connecting Northampton with Brackley. The latter was a daily service, whilst the 86 and 87 operated Monday to Saturday.

2012

A new service linking Northampton with the villages of Houghton, Denton, Cogenhoe, Bozeat and Wollaston commenced on 30 April. Route 43 was introduced by Finedon-based Roy's Minibuses, operating Mondays to Saturdays.

Country Lion withdrew its route 18 (Weston Favell Centre–University of Northampton, Park Campus) from the 1 September 2012.

It was at this time that Uno Buses Limited of Hatfield set up an operation in Northampton, with services starting on the 1 September 2012. The vehicles were based at the University of Northampton's Park Campus on Boughton Green Road. From this date two routes commenced operation, the 18 (Weston Favell–Sunnyside, University Park Campus via Boothville and Moulton) and the 19 (Northampton Rail Station–Bus Station–University of Northampton Avenue Campus–Kingsley Park–Kingsthorpe–Sunnyside, Park Campus). The service was taken over from Country Lion, whilst the 19 was won from Souls of Olney.

15 October saw United Counties route X7 (Northampton–Market Harborough–Leicester) extended southwards to Milton Keynes. This, coupled with the X4, provided a more frequent link between Northampton and Milton Keynes.

2013

The Uno network in Northampton expanded in January 2013 when a third service was introduced. Numbered 21, this route operated between Northampton Bus Station, Kingsthorpe, Eastern Avenue and Park Campus. The introduction of this route saw ten buses per hour running between Northampton town centre and Park Avenue.

Meridian Bus introduced yet another local service in Northampton from 17 November. Numbered 20 the service operated from Kingsthorpe, Eastern Avenue North and Greyfriars on a Sunday. The route ceased operating at the beginning of July 2014.

On 24 March, United Counties introduced a couple of new services. The first was the 51 which linked Rectory Farm with Northampton on Mondays to Fridays. Seven journeys were provided on the service. The second was the 9B, providing a more direct link between Old Duston, Northampton town centre, Northampton General Hospital and the Weston Favell Centre. On 12 May, another new route was introduced, the 12, which operated between Kings Heath, town centre and Camp Hill and on 13 May another new route '10' between Shelfleys, Northampton town centre and Parklands was added. In June, route 3 was extended to Sunnyside. A new early morning and evening service, the 58, was introduced on 4 November between Northampton and Kettering. Other services were introduced by United Counties over the summer of 2013, these being noted below.

2013 was the final year of Northampton Transport after First Group decided to close the Northampton operation. From 9 June First Northampton de-registered routes 12 (Greyfriars–Camphill); 23 (Greyfriars–Casewell Road/Salthouse Road); 28 (Greyfriars–Mereway Tesco) and 29/30 (Kings Heath–Greyfriars), these being formally withdrawn in August, leaving routes 2, 4 and 4A. At the same time Stagecoach de-registered route 3, this route had run in competition with First Northampton. After this date, United Counties altered routes 16 and 17 to operate as cross-town services between Kingsthorpe, Greyfriars, Weston Favell Centre and Ecton Brook. The Kings Heath service of routes 29 and 30 was numbered 8 by United Counties. The route served Baring Road and Vicarage Road. The Gladstone Road section of the route was solely served by Britannia Buses' route 31. Route 23 was taken over by Country Lion, operating Monday to Fridays between Greyfriars and Brackmills Industrial Estate. Country Lion operated the route until it ceased in November 2018. The withdrawal of the above services left First Northampton operating routes 2, 4 and 4A.

It was formally announced on 11 July that First Northampton was to cease operation. From 10 August, route 4 (Greyfriars–Obelisk Rise) was withdrawn. The final two services ceased operation on 14 September. Route 15 was another service registered by United Counties, operating between Greyfriars and Acre Lane. This operated alongside First Northampton's route 4A, commencing operation in July. A Sunday service was also introduced on the route, unlike on the 4A. Route 2 was taken over by United Counties from 15 September, running over the same route as First Northampton.

2014

Centrebus introduced three new services from 1 September, all of which operated on Wednesdays and Saturdays only. Route 61 operated between Guilsborough and Northampton, whilst route 62 provided a link between Scaldwell, Brixworth and Northampton. The final service, the 63, ran between the White Horse, Norton and Northampton, via The Bringtons. The latter service gained a Monday service from 22 October 2017.

September 2014 saw Meridian Bus withdraw from route 31. It was taken over by new operator Britannia Bus Ltd, which was based in Carlton Colville, Suffolk. From 29 September, they took over route 31 between Severn Drive, Kings Heath and Northgate bus station.

In January 2014 a college day service between Rectory Farm and Northampton town centre was introduced, linking them with Weedon Bec and Daventry college, operating Monday to Friday term time. Another route was added to Uno's portfolio in November. Route 37 ran between Hannington Church and Northgate bus station.

The route was operated by Uno until the end of August 2015, when it passed to Centrebus.

The final service introduced by Meridian Bus of Potterspury commenced operation at the end of March. Route 29 ran between Greyfriars bus station, St James Square, Northampton rail station and Gladstone Road. The service lasted five months before being withdrawn in mid-August.

United Counties introduced new service 24 (town centre–John Dryden House) on 6 January. This provided a Monday to Friday peak time service to the latter destination. 2 March saw the withdrawal of the 36 between Northampton and Piddington.

In October 2014, the Northampton, Kettering and Corby garages operating on the United Counties licence were merged with Stagecoach Warwickshire garages at Rugby, Leamington Spa, Nuneaton and Stratford-on-Avon, all operating on the Midland Red South licence. From this date, Midland Red South's head office transferred from Rugby to Main Road, Far Cotton, Northampton. The Company continued to trade as Stagecoach Midlands. At the time of the transfer, local routes being operated were:

1 Northampton Bus Station–Rectory Farm
2 Northampton Bus Station–Rectory Farm
3 Rye Hill–Riverside via town centre
4 Northampton Bus Station – Obelisk Rise
5 Southfields–town centre–St Giles Park
7 Grange Park–University of Northampton
8/81 Silverstone–Bicester
8 Earls Barton–Silverstone, running via Rectory Farm, Northampton and Towcester
9/9A Northampton–Duston
9B Old Duston–Town Centre–NGH–Weston Favell Centre
10 Shelfley–town centre–Parklands
12 Kings Heath–town centre–Camp Hill
14 Horton/Piddington–town centre–East Hunsbury
15 Northampton–Acre Lane
16/16X/17 Ecton Brook–town centre–Holly Lodge Drive
22 St Giles Park–Northampton
22A Northampton–St Giles Park
24 Northampton–John Dryden House
50/50A Northampton Bus Station–Shelfleys
51 Brackmills–Northampton
53 Northampton–Brackmills.

At the same time, a number of country services were operating into Northampton:

38 Kettering–Northampton
58 Northampton–Moulton Park
54 Northampton–Moulton Park
86 Northampton–Towcester
87 Northampton–Towcester
89 Northampton–Milton Keynes
X4 Peterborough–Corby–Kettering–Wellingborough–Northampton–Milton Keynes
X7 Milton Keynes–Northampton–Market Harborough–Leicester
X46 Northampton–Wellingborough–Rushden–Thrapston

X47 Northampton–Wellingborough–Rushden–Thrapston
D1/D2/D3 Northampton–Daventry.

November 2014 saw Stagecoach Midlands introduce new workers' service 7 between St James Square and Moulton Park industrial estate, providing three journeys a day Monday to Saturday. Route 37 was also introduced in November operating between Hannington and Northampton, providing two journeys. Route 7 was cancelled in October 2016, with route 37 suffering the same fate in September 2015.

2015

A new service linking between Hannington, Mears Ashby, Weston Favell and Northampton was introduced at the end of August. Numbered 37, this service replaced the service mentioned above.

9 September 2015 saw Uno Buses Limited commence operation of three services to Moulton College. 801 ran from Bletchley, Milton Keynes, Stony Stratford and Roade to Moulton College; 802 from Milton Keynes and Newport Pagnell to Moulton whilst the third route, the 803, operated from Bedford to Moulton via Olney and Yardley Hastings, the vehicles being out-stationed at Uno's garage in Cranfield, Bedfordshire.

In September a new route between Towcester (Old Trafford Road Tesco) and Northampton was introduced by Country Lion. Numbered 87, the route also served Rothersthorpe, Pattishall and Greens Norton. This route lasted for just under three years, being withdrawn from 22 July 2018.

April 2015 saw Stagecoach Midlands withdrew routes 4 (Greyfriars–Obelisk Rise) and 22/22A (Greyfriars–St Giles). A new workers' service between Grange Park and Lumbertubs, numbered 57, was introduced in June 2015, following the various shift patterns of businesses on the estate. It lasted for two years, being withdrawn in June 2017.

2016

Britannia Bus Ltd introduced route 901 on 7 August, operating between Northampton bus station and The Cross, Lavendon. The villages of Brafield on the Green and Yardley Hastings were also served by this Sunday only route. It lasted for just over a year, being withdrawn at the beginning of November 2017.

Goode Coaches withdrew its last service to Northampton (289 Paulerspury High Street–Northampton) at the beginning of September. July 2016 saw Uno withdraw Moulton College services 801 to 803.

The first service change for Stagecoach Midlands in 2016 took place on 21 February when route 86 (Northampton–Towcester) was withdrawn. It was taken over by Uno, departing from The Drapery. It served the villages of Blisworth and Shutlanger, operating until July 2018 when it was withdrawn.

Further service changes took place in April. At this time a new route 8 was introduced between Rectory Farm, Northampton town centre and Kings Heath, replacing the service that ran between Northampton and Bicester. A second new service, the 88, commenced operation from 21 April, running between Northampton and Northampton College, this being withdrawn in January 2017. From mid-April, routes 38 and 39 (Northampton–Kettering) were withdrawn, as was route 14 (Horton/Piddington–town centre–East Hunsbury).

2017

The Market Harborough to Welford section of Centrebus service 60 was withdrawn from April 2017, the service continuing to run between Welford and Northampton. In October, the daily route 37 (Hannington–Mears Ashby–Northampton) was replaced by a new route 37 operating on Mondays, Wednesdays and Saturdays only. The route was also altered to operate between Mears Ashby, Weston Favell and Northampton.

Another Buckinghamshire-based operator commenced operation into Northampton from 30 October. Red Rose Travel of Aylesbury won the contract for the 33 and 33A (Central Milton Keynes–Wolverton–Hanslope–Roade–Wootton–Northampton, The Drapery) from Z & S International.

On Boxing Day 2017 Country Lion services in the town were withdrawn, these being the 6 and 108.

Two new local services were introduced by Stagecoach Midlands in 2017. The first began at the end of January; numbered 9, it ran between Brambleside and the town centre. 20 March saw the withdrawal of route 24. A new shopping complex opened in the summer of 2017 on the edge of Rushden, called Rushden Lakes. From 24 July, Stagecoach Midlands introduced a number of services linking various towns and villages in Northamptonshire to the new complex. RL1 was introduced to operate between Kings Heath, Northampton town centre, Weston Favell and Rushden Lakes Monday to Saturday. These services were not a success, with the RL1 being withdrawn in February 2018. New routes were introduced in September 2017, X90 (Northampton–Milton Keynes) and X44 (Wellingborough–Brackmills). The X90 provided one return journey, Monday to Fridays, whilst the X44 ran three trips in the mornings and three in the evenings. Stagecoach Midlands were successful in winning the contract for Amazon, running between Northampton and the Amazon distribution centre at Marston Gate, Bedfordshire. This commenced in September 2017, lasting until January 2018.

2018

Wellingborough-based Shire Community Transport commenced operation of a service named 'The Village Hopper'. This Monday to Saturday service operated between Church Street, Wellingborough and Northampton bus station. It served the villages of Wollaston, Bozeat, Grendon, Castle Ashby, Whiston, Cogenhoe, Brafield, Little Houghton and Great Houghton before passing through the Cliftonville area of Northampton. The service commenced operation on 23 July 2018, replacing Roy's of Finedon route 43 which was withdrawn.

Shire's involvement in the route was, however, short-lived. From 1 October, the service was taken over by the Cogenhoe & Whiston Parish Council, based in Grendon. From this date, the route gained number VH1 and continued to operate between the two termini mentioned above. However, the route was amended slightly to serve the villages of Wollaston, Bozeat, Easton Maudit, Grendon, Whiston, Cogenhoe, Brafield, Little and Great Houghton before continuing on to Northgate bus station.

The University of Northampton opened their new Waterside Campus located just off Bedford Road in the summer of 2018. This resulted in the cancellation of the original services in the town, and new services registered, these starting from 5 August. Route 18 operated between Sixfields and the Waterside Campus, gaining Foxglove branding. Route 19 operated between Park Campus, the town centre and Waterside Campus, gaining Violet branding. Route 20 operated a circular service from Waterside Campus, only lasting until the end of July 2019. The final route was the 21, which continued to operate between Rectory Farm and the town centre, branded Lilac.

Stagecoach Midlands introduced a service from 23 July 2018. The first was numbered 87 and ran between Northampton and Towcester.

2019

Britannia Bus Ltd expanded its operations during 2019, introducing three services. The first was numbered X89 and ran between Northampton and Watling Street, Towcester. Introduced on 7 January, it did not last long and was withdrawn by the beginning of April. Next to commence operation was the 86, starting on the 4 July. The route provided a link between Deanshanger, Cosgrove, Blisworth, Collingtree and Northampton. However, this new service only operated on Thursdays. The 86 was superseded by route 13, introduced on 1 July. This was a new local service in Northampton, operating from the town centre to Fulford Drive, Links View via Kettering Road.

Z&S Travel regained the contract for the 33 and 33A (Milton Keynes–Northampton) from Red Rose Travel from 21 July.

Some journeys on the VH1 service operated by the Cogenhoe & Whiston Parish Council were extended on Monday to Fridays to serve the Weston Favell Shopping Centre.

Centrebus withdrew from service 60 (Welford–Northampton) from 27 October. The service was replaced by one operated by Uno Buses.

A new service, the 17, was introduced to connect Weston Favell, Waterside Campus, town centre and Far Cotton in September. The route was branded Poppy, this being applied to Enviro 200s 528 and 529.

A handful of new services were introduced by Stagecoach Midlands from 6 January. Route 4 was introduced to run between the town centre and Holly Lodge Drive. At the same time, route 6 was introduced to run between the town centre and Camp Hill, with half hourly journeys serving Mereway Tesco. A circular service between Northampton town centre and Butts Road was also introduced. A day later saw the introduction of route 9C between Northampton, St James and Duston, operating morning only journeys Monday to Friday, as well as the withdrawal of routes 89 and X89 between Northampton and Potterspury. In July route 14 between Northampton town centre and Moulton was added. The final changes for 2019 were the introduction of route 11 between Grange Park and Northampton town centre.

2020–2021

2020

The 2020/2021 Covid 19 pandemic saw a number of changes to the bus industry, along with a reduction in the number of people using buses. A national lockdown started on 23 March 2020, seeing service reductions to Stagecoach Midlands' network, as well as the independent operators' services. Most operators were operating a skeleton service at this time, with many routes going hourly. Services started to pick up over the summer of 2020 once some restrictions were lifted. Uno also reduced its service levels from 30 March 2020.

On 24 December, Stagecoach Midlands withdrew routes 107 (Overstone–Moulton Park), 50 (town centre–Pineham) and 106 (St James–Moulton Park).

Two new community bus services were established in Northampton from 24 June 2020. These were operated by a company called Comm Minibus Limited of London, who established a garage in Wellingborough.

2021

Arriva the Shires returned to the Northampton area from the 1 April 2021 after they won the contract for routes 33 and 33A from Z & S Transport. The service continued to operate between Northgate Bus Station, Roade and Milton Keynes Rail Station and The Point.

Potterspury-based Britannia Bus Limited introduced a new Monday to Saturday local service in Northampton from 21 June. Numbered 34, the route started at Park Drive, Kings Heath and served Kingsthorpe Road, Kingsley Hollow, Morrisons and Churchill Avenue before reaching the Weston Favell Centre.

Uno altered the routeing of the 17 in October. This Monday to Friday service operated between Far Cotton and Northampton Town Centre, then continuing from Little Billing. A month earlier, the company introduced a service between the University of Northampton's Waterside Campus and Rushden Lakes. Branded as the Lakeline, the route was not well patronised and was withdrawn by February 2022.

Wellingborough-based Comm Minibus Limited introduced a third service into the Northampton area from 29 October 2021. Numbered 78D, the route provided a Friday only service between Mawsley Village, Kettering and the Weston Favell Centre.

Leyland bodied Leyland Titan PD2/12 was new to York Bros. in February 1952, taking rolling stock number 1. It is photographed travelling through Northampton bound for the Northamptonshire village of Bozeat. *794 Preservation Group*

190 (DNH190) was the first of five Roe bodied Daimler CVG6 double-decks to be delivered to Northampton Corporation in August 1953. It lasted in public service until 1969, at which time it was put to further use as a driver training vehicle, finally leaving the fleet in October 1978. It is photographed on The Drapery toward the end of its passenger service career. *794 Preservation Group*

210 (JVV210) was new to Northampton Corporation in May 1959. It is photographed on The Drapery whilst working route 3 to Eastern Avenue. *David Shadbolt*

214 (JVV214) was another Daimler CVG6 to arrive with Northampton Corporation in May 1959. It is captured by the camera heading down The Drapery whilst operating route 14 to Parklands. *David Shadbolt*

228 (ONH228) was one of six Roe bodied Daimler CVG6s to be delivered to Northampton Corporation in March 1962. It is seen on The Drapery bound for Mereway whilst on route 9. *David Shadbolt*

238 (RNH238) represents the 1963 deliveries, all arriving in March. It is seen on layover, blinded for its journey to St James, The Square. *794 Preservation Group*

The Drapery provides the backdrop to Roe bodied Daimler CVG6 247 – BNH247C. 247 was one of six CVG6s delivered to Northampton Corporation in March 1965 and is seen heading towards Gloucester Avenue whilst operating route 7. *David Shadbolt*

December 1966 251 (BNH251C) was the last of the 1965 deliveries to Northampton Corporation. It is seen leaving Greyfriars for Briar Hill. *Gary Seamarks*

December 1966 saw the arrival of six Roe bodied Daimler CVG6 double-decks numbered 252 to 257. The first member of the batch, 252 (ENH252D), is seen entering Abington Street on route 26 towards Briar Hill Estate. *David Shadbolt*

April 1967 saw the arrival of Duple bodied Ford R192 LBD49E with York Bros. it is seen below showing off the two-tone blue livery. *794 Preservation Group*

October 1968 saw the final five Roe bodied Daimler CVG6 double-decks enter the Northampton Corporation fleet. 265 (JVV265G) is seen entering Abington Street whilst on service 1 to Newtow Road. *David Shadbolt*

266 (JVV266G) was the penultimate Daimler CVG6 delivered to Northampton Corporation, arriving in October 1968. It is seen heading back to Northampton town centre on route 13. *794 Preservation Group*

Basford of Greens Norton operated a couple of routes into Northampton from west Northamptonshire. TNV599G, a Willowbrook bodied Ford R192, was one such vehicle to operate the routes, being new to the company in 1969. *794 Preservation Group*

The first full-size single-deckers to enter the Northampton Corporation fleet since 1932 did so in April 1972. NJW708E was one of two Strachan bodied AEC Swifts acquired from Wolverhampton Corporation Transport. Taking up rolling stock number 21, it is photographed on layover in St James Garage. *794 Preservation Group*

Twenty additional Daimler single-decks arrived with Northampton Corporation in 1972/1973. 5 (UNH5L) was delivered to the company in April 1973. It shows off the dual-door layout well. *794 Preservation Group*

The Drapery finds Daimler saloon 9 (UNH9L) heading for Headlands on route 4. *794 Preservation Group*

UNH14L was another member of the twenty-strong fleet of Willowbrook bodied Daimler saloons delivered to Northampton Corporation between December 1972 and April 1973. It is seen on route 19 to Mereway entering Abington Street. *David Shadbolt*

The last member of the batch of Daimler single-decks, 20 (UNH20L), is seen about to enter Greyfriars bus station having completed its journey on route 5. A United Counties Bristol VRT can be seen on layover in the background. *794 Preservation Group*

Duple bodied Volvo B58 JNV78L was new to York Bros. in July 1973. It is seen showing off the two-tone blue livery. *794 Preservation Group*

A year later, in April 1974, Plaxton bodied Volvo B58 RBD74M was purchased by Yorks Travel. It is seen below along with two West Midlands Travel double-decks. *794 Preservation Group*

Goode Coaches operated a number of local contract and school services in the Northampton area. 949AFC, a Park Royal bodied AEC Regent V, was new to the City of Oxford Motor Services. *J.S. Cockshott Archive*

Willowbrook bodied Bedford YRT 101 (RBD101M) is photographed on layover at Derngate Coach Station having completed a journey on route 302. *794 Preservation Group*

The Leyland National became the workhorse of many bus fleets in the UK during the 1970s and 1980s. Northampton Corporation took stock of twelve of the type in October 1974. The third member of the batch, 25 – PNH25N – is seen departing Greyfriars Bus Station on route 40 to Headlands. *794 Preservation Group*

34 (GNH598N) was numerically the last Leyland National in the Northampton Corporation fleet. 34 is photographed at the Weston Favell Centre whilst operating route 306. The 306 was jointly operated by Northampton Corporation and United Counties. *David Shadbolt*

62 (VVV62S) was one of a batch of Bristol VRTs purchased by Northampton Corporation in 1977. It is photographed on its approach to Greyfriars. *Gary Seamarks*

68 (VVV68S) was new to Northampton Corporation in November 1977. It is seen operating route 19 to Mereway having just travelled down the hill on Gold Street. *Gary Seamarks*

70 (VVV70S) was the last Bristol VRT to arrive with the Corporation in 1977, arriving in November. It is seen departing Greyfriars on route 2 towards Kings Heath. *794 Preservation Group*

The Bristol VRT also featured heavily in the United Counties fleet, the first arriving in 1969, the last new ones arriving in 1981. Bodywork on the United Counties VRTs was constructed by Eastern Coach Works (ECW). 878 (XNV878S) was the first of fourteen Bristol VRTs to be delivered to United Counties in February 1978. It is seen entering Greyfriars blinded for its journey to Irthlingborough. *Gary Seamarks*

The Leyland National became one of the standard single-deck buses used by the National Bus Company during the 1970s and 1980s. United Counties 561 KRP561V represents the type, arriving with United Counties in August 1979. *D.J. Hancock Collection*

LRP66V was a Plaxton bodied Ford R1114 new to Yorks in September 1979. It is seen operating route Y2 between Northampton and Irthlingborough. In August 1988, it was one of two vehicles to transfer to United Counties when the latter operator took over the service. *794 Preservation Group*

The former Greyfriars Bus Station provides the backdrop to this photograph of ECW bodied Bristol LHS6L 21 (KBD21V), one of two such vehicles delivered to Northampton Corporation in October 1979. It is seen on the start of its journey on route 6 to Dallington Green. *794 Preservation Group*

Roe bodied Daimler CVG6 261 (GNH261F) became the last normal crewed vehicle in the fleet. It is seen after overhaul in 1981. *Laurence Knight*

Johnsons Coaches of Hanslope operated route 33 into Northampton for a number of years. The fleet is represented by FKX103K, a Willowbrook bodied Bedford YRQ new to the company in March 1972. *794 Preservation Group*

Setra S215H FSV305 was new to Yorks in May 1982, originally registered ENH92X. It is seen on layover in St Johns Street. It had gained the private registration mark by March 1985. *Matt Cooper*

East Lancs bodied Bristol VRT 73 (ABD73X) is seen passing through the grounds of the Tesco superstore located just off Mereway. 73 was new to Northampton Corporation in January 1982. *David Moth*

Six further Bristol VRTs arrived in late 1981, early 1982. This final batch of VRTs carried East Lancs bodywork. 75 (ABD75X) is seen inside St James Garage. *794 Preservation Group*

Ten of the twelve Leyland Nationals featured all-over advertising liveries during their careers with Northampton Corporation. 29 (GNH599N) gained one in April 1983 for Lindy's Bakeries Limited. It is seen on Sheep Street wearing this livery, bound for Headlands on route 5. *794 Preservation Group*

1984 saw six East Lancs bodied Leyland Olympians purchased by Northampton Corporation. 78 (A78RRP) arrived in March 1984 and is seen entering Greyfriars Bus Station whilst operating route 1. *794 Preservation Group*

82 (A82RRP) was the last East Lancs bodied Leyland Olympian delivered to Northampton Corporation in 1984. It is seen at Greyfriars whilst operating route 1 to Ecton Brook. *Gary Seamarks*

The late 1980s, early 1990s saw a number of Volvo B10M Citybus double-deckers delivered to Northampton Corporation. The first pair arrived in October 1986 and were the only ones to carry East Lancs bodywork. D102XNV was originally numbered 2, later gaining new fleet number 102. *794 Preservation Group*

Northampton Transport took stock of eight Alexander bodied Renault S56 minibuses in 1987/1988. The last of the eight, 110 – E110JNH – is seen approaching Greyfriars Bus Station whilst heading towards Lumbertubs on route 6. *794 Preservation Group*

ECW bodied Bristol VRT 830 (HRP670N) was the only vehicle to arrive with United Counties in May 1975. It is seen entering Greyfriars wearing the green and orange/cream stripes applied to the United Counties fleet post-National Bus Company ownership. *Gary Seamarks*

July 1988 saw the arrival of the first East Lancs bodied Volvo B10M. Numbered 111 (E111NNV), it is seen in Northampton whilst operating one of the summer Saunterbus services on behalf of Northamptonshire County Council. *Gary Seamarks*

York Bros. took stock of a number of Kassbhorer Setra S215 coaches during the 1980s. XLC516 was new as B87GBD in 1985 before being re-registered in 1988. It is seen loading in The Drapery. *794 Preservation Group*

84 (F84XBD) was one of three Alexander RV bodied Volvo B10M Citybus double-deckers delivered to Northampton Transport in May 1989. It is seen passing through the Weston Favell Centre, heading towards Duston. It is seen carrying writing celebrating 800 years of the Northampton town charter. *Gary Seamarks*

The X61 ran between Leicester, Market Harborough and Northampton. It was jointly operated by United Counties and Midland Red (East) Ltd, later Midland Fox. C30EUH, an East Lancs bodied Leyland Olympian, was operated by Midland Fox and is seen entering Greyfriars having just completed a journey on the X61. *Gary Seamarks*

F112YVV was one of the smaller vehicles in the Yorks fleet. This Ford Transit was new to the company in February 1989, gaining fleet number 12. *794 Preservation Group*

The first new double-deckers to enter the United Counties fleet after being purchased by the Stagecoach Group came in the form of the Alexander RL bodied Leyland Olympian. 622 (F622MSL) was one of this batch, being allocated to Northampton for use on route 51 (Duston–town centre–Blackthorn), which gained the Great Eastern Line branding. It is seen passing through the Weston Favell Centre. *Gary Seamarks*

1988 and 1989 saw twenty-eight ECW bodied Bristol VRTs acquired by United Counties from Devon General. 749 (LFJ866W) was one allocated to Northampton and is captured by the camera at the Weston Favell Centre bound for Higham Ferrers on route 46. *Gary Seamarks*

1982 saw fifteen ECW bodied Leyland Tiger coaches purchased by United Counties for Express work. They were later used on the Coachlinks network introduced during May 1986; the brand being carried on by Stagecoach when they took over United Counties in 1987. 176 (CNH176X) is seen departing Greyfriars wearing the Stagecoach stripe livery, relieved by Coachlinks fleet names. *Gary Seamarks*

Twenty ECW bodied Leyland Olympians arrived with United Counties in 1981 and 1982. 609 (ARP609X) was part of this batch. It is seen in full Stagecoach stripe livery parked at Greyfriars. *Matt Cooper*

United Counties took a number of second-hand ECW bodied Bristol VRTs into stock during the late 1980s, early 1990s. KRU847W was new to Hampshire Bus, and was acquired by United Counties in January 1988, taking fleet number 973. It is seen wearing the Stagecoach stripe livery whilst paused on The Drapery. *794 Preservation Group*

Alexander RV bodied Volvo B10M Citybus 93 (H293VRP) arrived with Northampton Transport in August 1990. It is seen on Upper Mounts departing the town centre for Rectory Farm. It is followed by United Counties ECW bodied Bristol VRT 936 (SNV936W) and an all-Leyland Olympian operated by Viscount, heading to Peterborough on the X65. *Laurence Knight*

June 1990 saw the arrival of a Caetano bodied Toyota HB31R with Yorks. This smart vehicle carried registration mark G118SNV and operated with Yorks until 1996. *794 Preservation Group*

Johnson's of Hanslope operated route 33 between Milton Keynes and Northampton for a number of years. Duple bodied Leyland Tiger THH616S is seen departing Greyfriars bound for Milton Keynes. *Gary Seamarks*

Alexander provided the bodywork for the remaining thirty Volvo B10M Citybus double-deckers purchased by Northampton Transport. 96 (J296GNV) is photographed in Duston whilst on route 1. 96 can be seen sporting the name 'Becketts Well'. *794 Preservation Group*

Midland Fox jointly operated the X61 between Northampton and Leicester. The route was predominantly operated by single-decks. However, on this occasion Alexander bodied Leyland Fleetline SHE545S is seen travelling out of Northampton on Harborough Road. *Laurence Knight*

Yorks took a pair of Van Hool Alizee bodied Volvo B10M coaches into stock during February 1992. ESK896 (originally D611MVR) represents the pair, taking stock number 52. *794 Preservation Group*

Basford of Greens Norton operated a couple of routes in Northampton, along with some school services. Former Northampton Transport VVV66S is seen on Towcester Road, Greens Norton. *Matt Cooper*

123 (K123URP) was one of six Volvo B10M Citybus double-decks to be delivered in September 1992. It is seen about to enter Greyfriars whilst on route 4 to Headlands. *794 Preservation Group*

132 (K132GNH) was the last Alexander bodied Volvo B10M Citybus double-deck to be purchased by Northampton Transport. It is captured by the camera on Kettering Road, heading towards Northampton town centre on route 5. *Laurence Knight*

The Alexander Dash bodywork became a popular choice with the Stagecoach Group during the 1990s, being offered on the Volvo B6 and Dennis Dart chassis. Between 1993 and 1994 United Counties took stock of thirty-eight Volvo B6 saloons with this bodywork. However, a small batch of Alexander Dash bodied Dennis Darts were taken into stock at Northampton in 1993 for route 85. 452 (K106XHG) represents this batch. *D.J. Hancock Collection*

The Olympian became the standard double-deck purchased by United Counties during the 1980s and 1990s. 682 (L682HNV) was one of fourteen Northern Counties Palatine I bodied Volvo Olympians delivered in August 1993. It is seen heading towards Duston on route 51. *D.J. Hancock Collection*

Plaxton Premiere 350 bodied Volvo B10M 96 (J450HDS) was numerically the last of a batch of five acquired by United Counties in April 1993 to update the fleet used on National Express contracts. It is photographed on layover inside Greyfriars. *Matt Cooper*

Trinity Bus and Coach of Brackley entered the Northampton bus scene in November 1994, starting up a town service between the town centre, Weston Favell Centre and Ecton Brook in competition with United Counties. For the route they used a fleet of Ford Transits, represented by C485TAY. *794 Preservation Group*

The GRT influence was seen during the mid-1990s, mostly through the livery worn by the fleet operated by Northampton Transport at the time. 25 (GMS297S) was new to Alexander (Midland) before passing to Leicester Citybus and then Northampton Transport in 1996. It is seen departing the gloomy Greyfriars Bus Station on route 27 to St Giles Park. *794 Preservation Group*

Plaxton Paramount bodied Volvo B10M XVY392 was new to Stainton, Kendal as B196MAO. It was acquired by Yorks in April 1995 and is seen on layover on Victoria Street before departing for nearby Cogenhoe. *Matt Cooper*

A trio of Alexander Ultra bodied Volvo B10L saloons arrived in October 1995. The last of the trio (41 – N41RRP) is seen attending the Showbus 1996 rally. *Gary Seamarks*

June 1997 saw the arrival of six somewhat unsuccessful gas buses with First Northampton. The first of the batch, 44 (P501MVV), is seen heading to Kingsthorpe, Acre Lane on route 30 wearing the special grey livery applied to the six Alexander Ultra bodied Volvo B10Ls. 44 was originally number 501. *Gary Seamarks*

A trio of Alexander Dash bodied Dennis Dart saloons entered the United Counties fleet during December 1996. 452 (P452KRP) was the last of the three saloons and is captured by the camera on layover at Greyfriars. *Matt Cooper*

Northampton was the first Stagecoach United Counties garage to receive low-floor vehicles. The first arrived in October 1998 in the form of nine Alexander ALX200 bodied Dennis Dart SLFs. The final member of the initial batch, 461 (S461CVV), is seen on The Drapery, operating route 15A to Wootton. They carried Lo-liner branding as seen above. *Matt Cooper*

Plaxton bodied Volvo B10M NTL655 was part of First Northampton's private hire fleet. It wore an all-over white livery and is seen on St Gregory's Road close to Booth Lane College. *Matt Cooper*

Northern Counties bodied Dennis Falcon 628 (C108SDX) arrived from Leicester Citybus in April 1997. It seen on its way to Rectory Farm. *794 Preservation Group*

Country Lion was heavily involved with school work with the Northampton and surrounding areas. They were also used on other private hire work, as well as rail replacement work. Irizar bodied Scania L94IB is photographed whilst on rail replacement, on layover in Milton Keynes. *794 Preservation Group*

Milton Keynes rail station provides the backdrop to this photograph of Plaxton bodied Volvo B10M A17CLN. Like A8CLN, it is captured by the camera whilst operating rail replacement work. *794 Preservation Group*

Poynter's Coaches of Northampton commenced operation in June 1988, and has continued operating private hire contracts and school work in the Northampton area since. Jonckheere bodied Volvo B10M J573JUY shows off the basic livery of this operator. *794 Preservation Group*

M8HCT is another member of the Collingtree Coaches fleet, this time a Jonckheere Deauville bodied Volvo B10M. It is photographed parked at the coach park in Central Milton Keynes. *794 Preservation Group*

Noge bodied MAN 18.310 R638VNN arrived with Yorks in May 1998 along with two other similar vehicles. It is photographed outside the Yorks Travel shop on The Drapery. *794 Preservation Group*

Collingtree Coaches commenced operation in January 1999, operating various private contracts within the local area. G51WPF, a Plaxton Paramount bodied Volvo B10M coach, shows off the basic livery worn by the fleet. *794 Preservation Group*

The First Northampton fleet was updated during the first part of 1999, with three Scania L94UBs arriving in January from First Leicester and a similar number of Scania L113CRLs, all carrying Wright bodywork. Scania L94UB 360 (S360MFP) is seen loading on The Drapery before heading towards Shelfleys. *794 Preservation Group*

December 1999 saw the arrival of three Wright bodied Scania L94UBs. They are represented by 362 (V362DNH), photographed paused on The Drapery. *794 Preservation Group*

Alexander bodied MCW Metrobus 265 (ULS637X) arrived with First Northampton in March 1999 from Leicester Citybus. It is seen at Spinney Hill Hall. *Matt Cooper*

A pair of Northern Counties bodied Volvo B6 saloons arrived from Capital Citybus in September 1999. 434 (L6GML) is seen approaching Greyfriars wearing a revised First Bus livery. *Gary Seamarks*

Y664NAY, a Marcopolo bodied MAN 24.400, was new to Yorks in April 2001. It is seen representing the company at the UK Coach Rally in Brighton. *794 Preservation Group*

Four Alexander bodied Leyland Atlanteans were sourced from First Aberdeen in May 2001 for use on school contracts. 331 (XSS331Y) is seen in Sheep Street, carrying the livery of its former owner. *Matt Cooper*

June 2001 saw the arrival of a pair of East Lancs bodied Dennis Dominators from Leicester Citybus. 148 (G667FKA) is captured by the camera at John Dryden House. *Matt Cooper*

Alexander Dash bodied Volvo B6 426 (L103PWR) entered the First Northampton fleet in October 2001. It is photographed at Links View wearing the 'Barbie 2' livery. *Matt Cooper*

Six Northern Counties Paladin bodied Dennis Falcon saloons arrived from Leicester Citybus in April 2002. The last of the batch, 626 (L626XFP), is seen loading on The Drapery before heading to Mereway. *Ben Everitt*

A pair of ECW bodied Bristol FLFs were acquired from Cambus in May 2002. They were soon repainted to celebrate the Queen's Golden Jubilee. 453 (JAH553D) was one half of the duo and is seen sporting the special livery whilst loading at the Weston Favell Centre. *Matt Cooper*

First Northampton received twenty-five nearly-new Wright Eclipse bodied Volvo B7Ls from First Manchester in September 2002. These had been used on work for the Commonwealth Games in Manchester over the summer. 342 (MV02VBE) is seen on the approach to Greyfriars, carrying Overground branding. *Gary Seamarks*

FN02HGU was a Marcopolo bodied Dennis Javelin coach operated by Yorks. It was new to the company in August 2002. *794 Preservation Group*

Collingtree Coaches operated the inter-campus shuttle on behalf of the University of Northampton. K828HUM is seen carrying branding for this contract. *794 Preservation Group*

Meridian Bus of Potterspury operated route 86 between Kings Heath and Northampton town centre. An Alexander Sprint bodied Mercedes-Benz 709D is photographed on The Drapery. *Author*

Poynter's Bova Futura YE03VSV is captured by the camera whilst paused in Bedford town centre. *794 Preservation Group*

Stagecoach have operated a shuttle service to the British Grand Prix since the early 1990s. A number of vehicles are hired from sister Stagecoach operations, running several routes to Silverstone from nearby sites. 16686 (P686JBD) is seen loading at Silverstone. *Matt Cooper*

The First Northampton fleet was renumbered in April 2004. 351 (MV02VBV) became 66333 to fit in with similar vehicles operated by First South Yorkshire. It is seen passing 66345 (MV02VCY) on The Drapery whilst operating route 28. *Author*

Five Dennis Dart SLFs arrived with United Counties from Stagecoach London in the opening months of 2005. 34097 (S497BWC) was one of three to carry Alexander ALX200 bodywork. It is seen loading on The Drapery, carrying branding for route 14 (East Hunsbury–Town Centre). *Author*

2005 saw competition arise between First Northampton and United Counties. The latter company had introduced a number of low-floor buses to its fleet by this time, whilst First Northampton were operating a number of step-entrance double-deckers. The spring of 2005 saw nine Wright Eclipse Gemini bodied Volvo B7TLs enter service with First. 32630 (KP54KBE) is seen heading to Sunnyside on route 4. *Liam Farrer-Beddall*

The Geminis were joined in May 2005 by ten Wright Eclipse Urban bodied Volvo B7RLE saloons. 66965 (KX05MJF) is seen about to enter Greyfriars, passing through on route 2 to Rectory Farm. *Author*

First Wyvern also provided a handful of Plaxton Verde bodied Dennis Lance saloons. 67237 (L237AAB) is captured by the camera on The Drapery whilst operating route 12. *Author*

A handful of Optare Solos were acquired from First Wyvern. 53050 (VU03YKD) represents the batch and is seen paused on The Drapery whilst on route 22. *Author*

A courtesy bus service was introduced by Country Lion between Northampton town centre and Beacon Bingo in 2006. Marshall bodied Dennis Dart SLF P4CLN is seen on The Drapery wearing a dedicated livery for the service. *Author*

The Optare Solo featured heavily in the MK Metro fleet, with 35 being operated by the company by the mid-2000s. 24 (YN53SVG) is seen in the yard of St James garage during the launch of the Buzz Card on 23 January 2006. It is seen carrying route branding for Northampton route 11. *Matt Cooper*

M K Metro Optare Solo 12 (V412UNH) is seen heading towards Northampton bus station on local route 22. *Author*

A number of Dennis Darts and Dart SLFs were also operated by MK Metro in the Northampton area. 62 (T408LGP) is seen paused on Sandy Lane. *Matt Cooper*

In addition to local bus work, MK Metro were successful in winning the contract for National Express route 455 between Northampton and London Victoria. Three Caetano Levante bodied Scania K340EB coaches were purchased for the route. The last of the trio, 4103 (FJ07TKF), is seen entering Greyfriars having completed its journey from London. *Liam Farrer-Beddall*

2009 saw National Express routes 302 (Northampton – Bristol) and 707 (Northampton – Gatwick Airport) pass to MK Metro, with an additional six Caetano Levante coaches being taken into stock, this time on the Scania K340EB4 chassis. 0420 (FJ09DXL) is seen at journeys end about to enter Greyfriars. *Liam Farrer-Beddall*

Twelve Enviro 300 bodied MAN 18.220 saloons were purchased by United Counties in April 2009 for route 1. 22832 (KX09BGU) is seen exiting North Gate heading towards Rectory Farm carrying full route branding. *Liam Farrer-Beddall*

Arriva MK Metro was another Buckinghamshire operator to operate route 33/33A between Northampton and Milton Keynes. ADL Enviro 300 3576 (KX09GZE) is seen dropping passengers off on The Drapery. *Liam Farrer-Beddall*

September 2010 saw Souls of Olney commence operation of three routes centred on the University of Northampton's Park Campus. Transbus Enviro 300 SN04EFH is seen carrying route branding for this service whilst paused on The Drapery. *Liam Farrer-Beddall*

A pair of former London Alexander ALX400 bodied Dennis Tridents were also used by Souls of Olney on the University of Northampton services. Former Stagecoach London V135MEV is seen carrying an all-over livery for the university whilst departing Greyfriars. *Liam Farrer-Beddall*

Transbus Pointer Dart EG02NZE is seen rounding Greyfriars carrying an all-over advertisement for the University of Northampton. *Liam Farrer-Beddall*

Country Lion commenced operation of route 11 (town centre–Parklands) in 2010. Enviro 200 CN06HOL is seen departing Northgate bound for Parklands. *Liam Farrer-Beddall*

2010 saw the Centrebus Group acquire Judge's Coaches of Corby. Route 60 (Northampton–Welford–Guilsborough) transferred to Centrebus. Former Stagecoach United Counties Optare Solo KX55PFO was numbered 231 in the Centrebus fleet. It is seen on the start of its journey to Guilsborough. *Liam Farrer-Beddall*

May 2011 saw Z & S Travel of Aylesbury take over route 33/33A. ADL Enviro 200 VE58XKY represents the company. It is seen loading passengers on The Drapery. *Liam Farrer-Beddall*

The remnants of the former Midland Red service X96 can still be seen in Northampton, operating as the 96. The route now runs between Northampton and Rugby. 36209 (KX60LHP) is seen carrying route branding for the service. *Liam Farrer-Beddall*

2011 saw the X4 (Milton Keynes–Northampton–Kettering–Peterborough) upgraded to a Gold service. For this a high specification batch of ADL Enviro 400 bodied Scania N230UDs were allocated to Kettering. 15747 (KX61DLO) is photographed paused at traffic lights at the top of The Drapery. *Liam Farrer-Beddall*

Roy's of Finedon started a new service linking Northampton with the villages of Houghton, Denton, Cogenhoe, Bozeat and Wollaston in 2012. Former Stagecoach United Counties Optare Solo KX55PEO was acquired by Roy's for use on the service. It is seen reaching journeys end at Northgate bus station. *Liam Farrer-Beddall*

Seven Mercedes-Benz Citaro saloons (301-7) were originally used on the 21 until they were replaced by older Dennis Dart SLF saloons. 301 (BX56VSJ) is seen on layover at the University of Northampton's Park Campus. *Liam Farrer-Beddall*

Route branding was applied to the majority of the Plaxton Pointer bodied Dennis Dart SLF saloons used by Uno on the 21. This is shown by 117 (C17UNO), leaving Northgate for Park Campus. *Liam Farrer-Beddall*

Route 19 was originally operated by a pair of Optare Solos numbered 401 and 402. However, from time-to-time other Uno buses from the Hatfield allocation could be found in Northampton. This is shown by Optare Solo 409 (YJ55YGE), branded for the St Albans Pink network in Hertfordshire. *Liam Farrer-Beddall*

A handful of former London United Alexander ALX400 bodied Dennis Tridents were operated by Uno in Northampton. 284 (SN51SYY) was one of these vehicles which is seen about to pass Northgate bus station. *Liam Farrer-Beddall*

Other vehicles were drafted in from Hatfield as the need arose. Transbus President bodied Trident 272 (PN03ULZ) is also seen about to pass Northgate. *Liam Farrer-Beddall*

The Transbus Trident featured heavily in the Stagecoach Northampton fleet over the years, with both new and second-hand examples being operated. 18153 (PX04DPK) was new to Stagecoach North West. It is seen loading on The Drapery whilst operating route 7. *Liam Farrer-Beddall*

A swap was made between First Northampton and First Eastern Counties in 2012. The Wright Eclipse bodied Volvo B7Ls moved to the latter operator, with Wright bodied Scania L113CRLs passing to First Northampton. 65554 (R554CNG) represents the batch and is seen rounding Greyfriars on route 28. *Liam Farrer-Beddall*

The fleet of Dennis/Transbus Darts at Northampton were replaced in 2014 by a fleet of thirty-seven AD Enviro 200 saloons. 37052 (YY63YPT) is seen departing North Gate bound for Rectory Farm on route 8. *Liam Farrer-Beddall*

Cambus Limited took over the Bedford operations of United Counties in October 2013. From this date route 41 was transferred, operating between Bedford, Olney and Northampton. Transbus Pointer Dart 34430 (KV53EZG) is seen on layover at North Gate bus station carrying Bedford Bus branding. *Liam Farrer-Beddall*

Britannia Buses commenced operation of the 31 between Northampton town centre and Kings Heath in September 2014. The company was formerly known as Meridian Bus. Over the years they have operated numerous vehicles on the route including Optare Solo SR KX14FHZ. It is seen departing Northgate bound for Kings Heath. *Liam Farrer-Beddall*

Whilst the Optare Solo was the common type used on route 60, Enviro 200s were also used on the route. 517 (YX63ZVT) is seen departing Greyfriars shortly after being delivered to Centrebus. *Liam Farrer-Beddall*

Chalfont Coaches of Southall won the contract for several National Express contracts in the Northampton area at the expense of MK Metro in 2013/2014. They gained a new operators' licence in the name of Chalfont Coaches, Northampton, establishing a base in Cogenhoe. Van Hool Alizee bodied Volvo B10BT WA10ENL is seen at Greyfriars having just operated a journey on the 455 from London. *Liam Farrer-Beddall*

2014 saw the arrival of a number of Caetano Levante bodied Volvo B9Rs. BK14LFA is seen passing Mayorhold car park bound for Gatwick Airport on the 707. *Liam Farrer-Beddall*

Country Lion commenced operation of route 87 (Northampton – Towcester) in 2015, the route continuing until 2018 when it was withdrawn. Optare Solo CN03HOL is seen leaving The Drapery bound for Towcester. *Liam Farrer-Beddall*

By 2016 Roy's of Finedon had replaced the Optare Solo on the Northampton to Wollaston service with a pair of former East Yorkshire Motor Services Plaxton Primo bodied Enterprise Plasma saloons. YX06HVK is seen at the start of its journey to the East Northamptonshire village of Wollaston. *Liam Farrer-Beddall*

2013 saw routes X46 and X47 upgraded to Gold status. 15936 (YN63BYB) was one of the fleet of AD Enviro 400 bodied Scania N230UDs to convert the route. It is seen heading to Kings Heath on the short-lived 2016 RL1 service to Rushden Lakes. *Liam Farrer-Beddall*

Red Rose Travel was a second Aylesbury-based operator to take on operation of routes 33 and 33A, taking them over from Z & S Travel in October 2016. AD Enviro 200 YX64VRK is seen completing its journey from Milton Keynes. *Liam Farrer-Beddall*

2015 and 2016 saw Uno invest in the single-deck fleet at Northampton, purchasing a number of Enviro 200 saloons. 519 (YX65RNN) was one of the 2015 batch and is seen blinded for its journey to Towcester on route 86. *Liam Farrer-Beddall*

525 (YX66WGY) represents the 2016 deliveries and is seen on its approach to Northgate bus station, blinded for its return journey on route 21 to Park Campus. *Liam Farrer-Beddall*

October 2017 saw the first of the Uno routes in Northampton rebranded. Route 19 gained the Violet name as seen on Enviro 400 MMC 292 (YX67VFW). *Liam Farrer-Beddall*

July 2018 saw Shire Community Transport of Wellingborough commence operation of a route between Northampton and Wellingborough, replacing a similar service operated by Roy's of Finedon. Ford Transit LF66YNR is seen on The Drapery carrying Village Hopper branding. *Liam Farrer-Beddall*

The Village Hopper service passed to Cogenhoe & Whiston Parish Council in October 2018. This brought with it a new Ford Transit minibus registered YT68ZSN. It is photographed having just departed Northgate bus station. *Liam Farrer-Beddall*

The Covid-19 pandemic saw the need for additional buses across many fleets around the United Kingdom. This allowed operators to adhere to the social distancing rules introduced by the Government. Stagecoach Midlands hired a number of double-deckers from Ensign Bus to help with this. Former Lothian Buses SN56AFA is seen leaving North Gate bus station on route 7, numbered 80077. *Liam Farrer-Beddall*

Arriva the Shires won the contract for the 33/33A between Milton Keynes, Roade and Northampton in April 2021, bringing the company back to Northampton. Whilst a range of vehicles could be found on the route, a pair of Wrightbus Streetlite WFs were the common vehicles to be found on the service. One of these, 2312 (LM64JNX), is seen on its loop round to its stand at Northgate bus station. *Author*

SOURCES

CARTER, Paul, *Premier Travel Ltd: A History*; Capital Transport; 1995
CRAWLEY, R.J., MACGREGOR, D.R., SIMPSON, F.D., *The Years Between 1909 – 1969: Vol. 1 The National Story to 1929*
Midland Counties News Sheets – Various issues
Notice & Proceedings: Eastern Area – Various issues 1970 – 2021; The Office of the Traffic Commissioner
PE14 Fleet History of Northampton Transport Limited; York Brothers (Northampton) Limited; Wesley's Tours (Northampton) Limited and their predecessors; PSV Circle; 1989
WARWICK, Roger, *An Illustrated History of United Counties, Vol. 1 – 17*
WARWICK, Roger, *Bygone Northamptonshire Buses*